Lost Souls: FOUND!™

Inspiring Stories About Pit Bulls

Kyla Duffy and Lowrey Mumford

Published by Happy Tails Books™, LLC

Happy Tails Books™ (HTB) uses the power of storytelling to effect positive changes in the lives of animals in need. The joy, hope, and (occasional) chaos these stories describe will make you laugh and cry as you go on a journey with these authors who are guardians and/or fosters of adopted dogs. "Reading for Rescue" with HTB not only brings further awareness to rescue efforts and breed characteristics, but each sale also results in a financial contribution to dog rescue efforts.

Lost Souls: Found!™ Inspiring Stories about Pit Bulls by Kyla Duffy and Lowrey Mumford

Published by Happy Tails Books™, LLC   www.happytailsbooks.com

The publisher gratefully acknowledges the numerous Pit Bull rescue groups and their members who generously granted permission to use their stories and photos.

The following brand names mentioned in this book are registered trademarks and the property of their owners. The author and publishing company make no claims to the logos mentioned in this book including: Hoover, Mack, Frisbee

Photo Credits (All Rights Reserved by Photographers):

Front Cover: Willow, Ashley Johnson, www.ashleyjohnsonphotography.com

Back Cover Top: Pam Marks, www.pawprincestudios.com

Back Cover L: Autumn, Teresa Oblak, www.olliephotography.blogsome.com

Back Cover Mid: Shana, Teresa Oblak

Back Cover R: Pam Marks

Inside Title: Pit Pack, Devlynn Saunders, www.rugazrescue.com

Publishers Cataloging In Publication

Lost Souls: Found!™ Inspiring Stories About Pit Bulls/ [Compiled and edited by] Kyla Duffy and Lowrey Mumford.

p. ; cm.

ISBN: 978-0-9824895-3-6

1. Pit Bull. 2. Dog rescue. 3. Dogs – Anecdotes. 4. Animal welfare – United States. 5. Human-animal relationships – Anecdotes. I. Duffy, Kyla. II. Mumford, Lowrey. III. Title.

SF426.5   2010

636.755   2009911457

Happy Tails Books appreciates all of the contributors and rescue groups whose thought-provoking stories make this book come to life. We'd like to send a special thanks to:

A Rotta Love Plus
http://arottalove.org/

Country Kennel Bully Rescue
http://www.countrykennelbullyrescue.com/

For the Love of Pits
http://www.fortheloveofpits.org/

For the Love of Dog
http://4theloveofdog.org/

Fugee's Rescue
http://www.fugeesrescue.org/

Hot Water Rescue New England
http://www.hotwaterrescue.com/

It's the Pits
http://www.itsthepits.org/

Linda Blair WorldHeart Foundation
http://www.lindablairworldheart.org/

New Hope Pit Bull Rescue
http://www.nhpbr.org/

Rugaz Rescue
http://www.rugazrescue.com/

The Buster Foundation
http://www.thebusterfoundation.rescuegroups.org/

Want more info about the dogs, authors, and rescues featured in this book? http://happytailsbooks.com

Table of Contents

Foreword: Angels Among Us

Growing up in Connecticut with a slew of woodland animals, dogs, cats, chickens, rabbits, horses, a pet skunk, and many wonderful cats, my childhood dream was to become a veterinarian. My mother explained to me that by working as a model, doing commercials, and acting in NYC, I could save my money and pursue my educational aspirations. So while my acting career flourished, I kept my love for animals close to my heart.

Losing Sheba, my sweet Jack Russell "best friend," who was stolen from my backyard in Southern California, changed my life and inspired me to get involved with animal rights (now known as animal welfare). Years later, after losing two beloved dogs and my mother, Elinore, within a two-and-a-half year period, I was unexpectedly pulled out of my sadness by a picture of a confused and desperate shelter dog in a cage, which provided me with a new mission: I didn't have to heal or find a new canine partner - I needed to lend a hand and foster a dog in need.

I found myself with a crazy Queensland Heeler/coyote mix, I guess, whose tormented emotional state seemed to rival my own. I told her that together we would heal each other. Her name was Missy, and after our three-month stay in NYC (while I made my Broadway debut in *Grease*), we returned to California.

One day we were walking home from the local park when a very large, brown and black brindle Pit Bull came sauntering out of the neighbor's driveway. Scared senseless because the news media had me convinced that Missy and I were looking certain death in the eye, I ran home, screaming at the dog to stay away. He neither picked up his pace nor displayed any of the evil, threatening, maniacal behavior the news media engraved in my head. When the dog casually laid down in my front yard, like any "normal" dog might, I realized something was wrong with this picture. So I approached him, and he smiled sadly, thumping his tail up and down, happy to see that I had not abandoned him. His chest was rubbed raw as if he had escaped from somewhere, and he seemed desperate for a friend. I offered him some water and introduced him to Missy, who was very interested in meeting him. I tried to find his guardian, but of course, he had none. So he followed me back home, begged to come inside, and after a fabulous, happy playtime with Missy, he curled up behind my lounge chair and fell asleep. I have never heard any human or dog snore so loudly in all my life—this poor guy was simply exhausted. I named him "Sunny Boy" for the sunshine and healing he brought to my sad heart, and he quickly became Missy's best friend and the dog who changed my life.

I began to get more involved with rescue, and one day an amazing, red and white, two-month-old, ball of Pit Bull puppy joy popped his head out of a dog run at the rescue where I was serving as president. He looked at me with hypnotizing green eyes and I was sold! This dog, Riley, was to become a key part in my campaign against Pit Bull slander, along with his brother Sunny.

Riley and Sunny have brought endless joy to my life, and my experience with them has been integral to learning more about Pit Bulls. Working with trainers has also taught me how to read behaviors and work with this breed. I now know them as well as I know myself!

Pit Bulls are the original American dogs: chosen as companions by several American war heroes, used in ads by Buster Brown and RCA, and portrayed as ideal family pets on television (like "Petey" from *The Little Rascals*). They are loyal, doing whatever their human tells them to do (right or wrong). They are active, playful, and intelligent comedians and couch potatoes. Extremely sensitive, they are similar to a two-year-old human child and a teenager, all at the same time.

Yet this wonderful breed is made to suffer in so many ways. Over-bred by backyard breeders, they are often weaned from their mothers too soon and sold to people like drug dealers and gangsters, who have no idea how to nurture them. They're babies, not macho status symbols. Abusive owners do horrible acts of cruelty to these dogs, like feeding them gun powder, depriving them of food and water, and beating them. They use weaker Pit Bulls as bait dogs to encourage stronger dogs to attack. When people ask me about fallen football "star" and known Pit Bull abuser Michael Vick, who electrocuted, drowned, and tortured animals to death for not being winning fighters, I say, "I needed his fame to prove I was telling the truth!" He's likely a man with anger and rage who is in desperate need of psychological help.

The point is that humans are responsible for what Pit Bulls are today. They were born and bred to be the most loyal companions, and people have taken advantage of this trait for cruel amusement and financial gain. The fact that these dogs save lives, and in some cases work as rescue dogs and drug-sniffing dogs, is rarely mentioned. Thanks to biased media and heartless people, our shelters are now filled with these amazing dogs who are always the first to be euthanized. *We* must change the way the public perceives Pit Bulls if they're ever going to surmount the current state of discrimination.

Being famous, I know what it is like to be misunderstood and, in some cases, to come face to face with prejudice. So how can I not fight to save these magnificent, misunderstood dogs? I now operate the Linda Blair WorldHeart dog rescue in Acton, CA, a property that is mostly filled with dancing, happy, grateful Pit Bulls, along with many other types of dogs as playmates. They're all waiting for a second chance to be adopted by a forever, loving home.

Pit Bulls came to me and asked for help years ago, and I have kept my word! And now I'm asking you to help me make a difference, one Pit Bull at a time. Let this important book, full of amazing stories about how the Pit Bull Terrier has changed people's lives, guide you in your thoughts and impressions about this misrepresented breed. Their compassion and joy shines through in every story, demonstrating the true, loving nature of Pit Bulls. I hope these passionate accounts will inspire you to lend a hand, whether that means donating to Pit Bull rescue, fostering, adopting, or simply correcting others who wish to slander these dogs. Every little bit counts, and each one of us who commits to correcting the way these dogs have been wronged will be another breath of wind that turns the tide of justice.

 *Linda Blair*

Inspiring Stories about Pit Bulls

*P*it Bulls, like Enzo (above), add precious moments to our lives. Social, energetic, and simply adorable, they're often the center of attention. Whether they are walking, fetching, or just licking us to pieces, Pit Bulls always seem to find a way to bring joy and laughter to those who care for and respect them.

Participating in Pit Bull rescue and adoption programs always has an amazingly positive impact on the dogs and on the families who adopt them. Ask any guardian of a Pittie and they'll tell you the same thing: "Not have a Pit Bull in my life? Mind boggling."

 Monique & Robert, Pittie Parents

Hit or Miss

I t's one of those random nights when class gets out early. It doesn't happen often in graduate school, so I take advantage of the opportunity and head home for some much-needed rest. Driving down the back roads, I see a dog up ahead to the left in the median. My heart skips a beat as the dog steps out into the three lanes of traffic and starts crossing the busy street. There's no way he's going to make it.

It happens in a flash—dog, traffic, slamming on my brakes, tires screeching, dog in front of my car, tears streaming down my face. Did I hit him? I think I hit him. I jump out of my car and look. He's not here. He's running down the street. I jump back into my car and follow him, but he crosses back over the six lanes of traffic. I quickly u-turn. He runs into a yard and, slamming my car into park, I run as it rocks to a stop. I follow him through several yards, finally catching up to him. He's a fairly large dog, scarred, dirty, and rough around the edges - a Pit Bull—maybe used as a bait dog. I approach slowly and quietly, whispering that everything is going to be okay. He meets me halfway - head down, tail between his legs.

A woman comes out of the house and asks if it's my dog. I tell her no, but I think I may have hit him with my car and need to be sure he's unhurt. I don't know much Spanish but I certainly understand when she says, "Loco." I move closer and let him sniff me, reaching my hand out to pet his sides. He doesn't appear hurt, but I can't be too sure. The woman's neighbor directs me to a local shelter.

We arrive at the shelter and the workers say they will take him in, send him to a vet, and once healthy, bring him back to the shelter. But if no one comes for him within seven days, he becomes at risk for euthanasia. I put my name down as a contact; the sweet dog didn't die in front of my car, so there is no way I am going to let him die in the shelter.

I'm so nervous to leave him, especially after the employee makes some comment about not liking Pit Bulls and requires me to take him out of my car and put him in the transport vehicle myself. He is such a good boy, though obviously scared, and my eyes well with tears again as I load him up.

An hour after I get home from my unexpected ordeal, I call the vet he was sent to, who reassures me that the dog has only sustained minor injuries from the accident. He's running a fever and severely dehydrated (likely from roaming the streets for days), but he's going to be fine.

The dog returns to the shelter the following day and is put into a run with two other dogs. This proves to be a bad idea as a fight subsequently breaks out, and "my" dog is yet again injured—now with torn ears and wounds on his back. He's blamed for the incident, deemed aggressive, and placed alone, even though nobody can really determine who started it.

His clock is ticking now that he's back at the shelter, and I visit him nearly every other day. I check regularly to see if his owners have come to claim him (if he has any). Nothing. Seven days go by and they tell me he will be euthanized. I'm absolutely beside myself and beg for more time, while I try to figure something out.

I can't bring him home (my roommate wants no part of it), and I'm turned down time after time by rescue groups: they are full; they don't take Pit Bulls; they don't take injured dogs; they don't take dogs from private parties. Some don't respond at all. It seems like hundreds of phone calls and emails before I finally connect with a wonderful woman named Ranelle, who seems to know everything and anything about the process of rescuing a dog from the Los Angeles shelter system. She gives me great guidance and says if I can pull the dog and board him, I can show him at the adoption events she holds. She hooks me up with a boarding facility that gives discounts to rescues... and our next adventure begins.

Following Ranelle's instructions, I pull Dodger, who I name after his vet visit near Dodger Stadium, and take him to Bark Avenue for boarding until I can find him a home. Dodger cleans up quickly after his first bath at Bark Avenue, and I get him toys, a collar, and a soft bed (which he promptly eats, along with the walls, during his first night at Bark - sorry guys!). Despite a rescue discount, boarding Dodger is still pretty pricey for a girl who is working full-time and putting herself through graduate school, so I start fundraising to help offset the cost. I'm amazed at all the wonderful people who help me out.

Dodger turns out to be an amazing dog, and everyone quickly falls in love with the big knucklehead. I find myself at Bark several times a week to walk him, snuggle with him, and convince him I'll find him his forever home. He's antsy around other dogs, and I'm not sure if he could become aggressive, so we enroll in the free Pit Bull training offered by Tia of Villalobos at the South Los Angeles Shelter. We go every weekend we don't have an adoption event, and Dodger grows less and less anxious.

Dodger and I have many adventures and mishaps over several months, drawing us very close. Though I think it bothers me more than him, my heart breaks each day I bring him back to the boarding facility. I love that dog more than anything and keep hoping we'll find him the perfect home.

It seems like forever, but Dodger finally gets a break. Drew, a friend of a friend, is interested; Dodger will have the run of his entire house and yard. So after a crazy spring and summer of training and adoption events, Dodger finally finds his forever home. I walk out the gate, crying just as hard as I had the day I met him, but this time they are tears of joy.

 *Kelli Doré*

Lady Liberty

I t wasn't long after the tragic events of September 11th, 2001, that I chased a basketball up the driveway of an abandoned home near my parents' house while playing with some neighborhood kids. For two weeks no one had lived there, but when the ball bounced off the garage door, a dog barked from inside the house. I walked over to the front window to peek in and, sure enough, there was a dog. Fortunately, the window had been left unlocked, so I opened it and pulled out a terrified female Pit Bull. She was shivering and extremely skinny from obvious malnourishment.

It was then that I noticed she wasn't the only animal inside—there was also this tiny, malnourished calico kitten. How amazing that as hungry as the dog was, she stuck beside her friend the kitten; it seemed she would have died before eating her pal.

The dog's name came quickly and naturally—freeing her from her "grave," coupled with the nation's (and my own) patriotism after September 11th—this dog was Freedom. I first gave her food and water, which she ate and drank in desperation. It saddened me that every time I would pet her gently on her head she immediately cowered to the ground as if expecting to get hit. The next day we visited the vet, who said other than needing to be "fattened back up," Freedom was in surprisingly good condition. Shortly thereafter, she came down with a horrific uterine infection, but $1,000 later she was as good as new.

I still have her today, my happy, lazy girl. The life of a couch potato, lounging around in air conditioning, suits her well. At about 12 years old now, she does have arthritis and allergies, but she's living the life of a queen...just as she should be. Let Freedom ring.

Eric Emminger

Bustered

L et me introduce you to Buster, a seventy-pound lapdog with the attitude and personality of Scooby Doo. He loves to eat, runs from danger, and will be your best friend for a few hugs and snacks. He was born at It's the Pits Rescue in San Diego after his mom was pulled out of an abusive situation. He weighed a measly thirteen pounds when we met him and I wasn't really looking to adopt that day, but Buster really picked us. My girlfriend (now wife), Lisa, and son fell in love with him instantly, so what's a guy to do?

I have to admit Buster is a very smart dog, as most Bullies are. He has learned to sit, speak, lay down, shake, and even eat on command. I was impressed at how quickly he learned to do things, but there was one person he loved to mess with: Lisa. I swear they have this funny, love-hate relationship thing going where they tease each other like crazy.

It was New Year's Eve and we had friends over at our house celebrating, so we crated Buster in the bedroom. As midnight approached we decided to go out to get coffee before counting down the New Year. Lisa stopped in the bedroom to check on Buster and say goodbye. She gently teased and laughed at him, since he is rarely crated in the house. He just smiled back, looking content.

Several hours passed, and with coffee cups emptied, we headed back home. As we arrived, Lisa noticed the blinds moving in our bedroom window and, of course, we were curious to see what the commotion was. We opened the front door and made our way into the bedroom to see Buster, innocently sitting inside his crate...with the room a total mess! Lisa had forgotten to lock the crate and Buster had wreaked havoc, now pretending that it had nothing to do with him. We were amazed at the chaos, but what caught our attention most was that he only destroyed Lisa's shoes. He ate two pairs of tennis shoes, one pair of heels, and one pair of flip-flops. In the end, Buster got the last laugh, and Lisa got new shoes.

What can I say, about these dogs? They are awesome when treated with love and respect. Despite his mischievousness, Buster is a great addition to our family and still messes with Lisa to this day. He always manages to find the one thing that drives her crazy, but in the end they look out for each other. Buster is part of our family: when times are tough he is always there, when you want someone to listen he won't talk back, and he is the first to lay in the middle of the kitchen floor so you can trip and drop your food for his enjoyment.

 Ahren Nunag

We have quite the rescued menagerie: three cats, two dogs, and a pot-bellied pig. Time and time again we've experienced the special bond that forms between rescued animals and their guardians—a different kind of love than what comes from an animal who was never really lost, abused, or neglected. So while bringing another dog into our lives would not fill the holes in our hearts left by the recent loss of our 15-year-old Lab, we knew we wanted to share our love with another dog in need.

Turning to Linda Blair's WorldHeart Foundation, we looked at and played with every beautiful dog at the rescue. We came very close to choosing a couple, but after almost an hour, Linda suddenly disappeared—returning momentarily with both a statement and a young dog. She said that after talking with us and getting what she thought was a pretty good feel, she determined we would be a perfect match with this little dog. The puppy appeared to have some significant neurological deficits, but Linda assured us that the dog was as sweet as could be.

She opened her arms, and out popped this silly-looking little Pitty—half-stumbling, ears flopping from one side to the other and then crossing over the top of her forehead, and each eye looking in opposite directions. Every time she shook her head she would lose her balance and fall over.

We sat in an enclosed area where she ran around at full speed, every once in a while swiftly jumping up on our laps to lay her head on our shoulders and then, just as suddenly, taking off running again. That was all it took; we were in love.

We brought her home, and as I sat down on the couch, she immediately jumped up to join me. Halfway across my lap she dropped, splayed across my legs and abruptly falling asleep. I decided this was too good an opportunity to miss and promptly lay down for a nap as well. When I awoke, there was this silly-looking, cross-eyed, lop-eared dog lying next to me, her nose pressed into my neck, her head on my arm and her body tight up against me. We were both content.

The name she came with was Rose, which was the name of one of my most favorite people—my Grandmother. We weren't sure if the name completely fit our new dog, but we kept calling her Rose, Rosie, etc. as she acclimated to her new surroundings. Then one day I whispered her name and

"Rosebud" just came out (yes, like in the movie *Citizen Cane*). It was in that instant that my wife and I looked at each other and decided it fit her best.

Rosebud has been with us for about six months now, and she has truly blossomed. We love the way she interacts with our other dog, a Rottie named Stan. She struts around after him, watching everything he does, and with that she has lost a significant part of those neurological disorders (although she does still wobble when she shakes her head too vigorously). She now protects our home, romps in the yard, and plays on the first step of our pool.

Like with our other rescues, again the bond has formed, and again there is a special kind of love that can only be experienced by providing for one who was truly in need.

 *Dr. Howard Maize*

Love Lifts the Veil of Fear

Peanut broke our hearts from the first moment we laid eyes on her. She was physically scarred with a constant look of fear. Her foster mother brought her over to see if our home would be a good fit for this poor little girl, and she would not come near us for fear we would harm her.

The visit with Peanut only lasted about 30 minutes, and then we had to make our decision whether to keep her. This was extremely tough because she acted as though she didn't want anything to do with us. As a dog lover I assumed she'd pick up on my good intentions, so I was surprised when she wasn't more affectionate towards me during our visit. My husband, on the other hand, was slightly intimidated because of her breed. The situation was shaky, but after a long night of debating, we decided that the best thing we could do for this precious girl was to take her into our loving home and give her a second chance at life. We thought we could turn Peanut's sad eyes into eyes filled with happiness and joy; Peanut deserved it.

It's been a year since we were given the gift of adopting Peanut through Hot Water Rescue, and what a wonderful difference she has made in our lives. She is the most loyal, gentle, and loving little girl anyone could ask for. There is never a moment where she doesn't want to cuddle up on our laps and sleep with us (or rather, between us), with her head on our pillow. She could easily have been named Cuddle Bug.

Before Peanut we never rushed home. Now we can't get home fast enough, just to see her smiling face running towards the door to greet us for belly rubs. It's amazing to think that the beginning of our relationship was shrouded by fear—hers of us because of her past experiences with humans and ours of her for being a Pit Bull—and now we are the happiest of families.

It is evident that Peanut is slowly forgetting her previous life on the streets: hungry, scared, and dirty. Now she is in a home where she is given constant love and affection, a place where she doesn't need to wonder where her next meal is coming from. Strangers still make Peanut anxious, but every day she gets braver and is slowly realizing no one will ever hurt her again. She is safe now, forever, and always.

Judy Tweedlie

A Sucker for Socks

A few years ago I lived with a friend who is one of the biggest animal lovers I have ever met. She somehow came up with the idea of volunteering at the local animal shelter, which has almost all Pit Bull mixes, and asked me whether I would like to do it with her. I enjoyed it so much that when she presented the idea of fostering some of the dogs until we could find them good homes, I was thrilled.

One dog in particular, Socks, had been extremely high-strung before we took her home. She circled frantically in her cage whenever anyone walked into the room, and when she finally did get out for her daily walk, she would sometimes pull so hard on the leash that she would choke herself. But my friend, who had an uncanny ability to choose which dogs needed fostering most, just knew that once we got Socks out of there she would be fine. We were barely a mile away from the shelter when Socks, who had been terrified to get in the car to begin with, let out a huge sigh and stretched out on the back seat, seemingly content. My friend and I couldn't help grinning.

It was always a pleasure to see the dogs' real personalities blossom as they got used to life away from the shelter, and Socks was no exception. She was very cuddly and affectionate and would actually slide over on the bed to make sure she was touching me when it was time to go to sleep. She caught on to the idea of pottying outside quickly (a relief!), but the concept of toys took her a little longer to grasp. The first time she picked up a squeaky tennis ball in her mouth and it let out an ear piercing squeal as she bit down on it, she dropped the ball and ran away from it, petrified.

Another friend came over to visit one evening and met Socks, who by that time had mastered playing with toys and loved showing everyone how she could make her ball squeak. My friend had already seen a picture of Socks and thought she was adorable. Suddenly she was powerless against Socks' charm. I left the two of them outside while I tended to the permanent canine resident of the house, and when I went back to get them they were nowhere to be found. Thirty minutes later the happy couple came wandering back from their impromptu walk, completely in love with each other.

This friend had been seriously contemplating adopting an animal. Her beloved cat, Gerry, had passed away a few months prior, and she was just getting to the point where she was thinking about adding to her family again. However, she had only ever had cats before and was unsure whether she was adequately equipped to handle a dog. For the rest of the evening, she peppered me with questions about dog care in general and what it might be like for her to share her home with Socks. Her biggest concern seemed to be whether or not she would be a good mom for Socks.

A few days later, after careful consideration, my friend made the decision that Socks was the pet for her. That was almost two years ago, and I am pleased to report that both my friend and Socks could not be happier. Socks has more toys than any other dog on the planet, which she takes great pleasure in squeaking at all hours of the day and night. I suspect Socks is proud of the fact that she's no longer afraid (I know *I'm* proud of her).

Socks has learned how to give hugs, which she will do for anyone and everyone whenever asked. She sleeps in bed with her mommy, despite the fact that Mom *swore* Socks would be confined to her own bed during the night (an edict that lasted all of 30 seconds). Her mom even indulges the fact that Socks is not a morning dog and lets her sleep in whenever possible. We discovered *that* fact the first morning we tried to take her out at the ungodly hour of *9:45am*. Socks peered blearily at us, made fake snoring noises and pretended she was still asleep. This was so cute we *had* to let her stay there until she was ready to go out.

My friend has since adopted another dog, an eight-month-old Pit Bull-mix named Clemmy, and Socks is the perfect big sister to the new addition to the family. I don't think Socks could possibly have ended up with a better home, and when I see her this afternoon, I'll ask her what she thinks. I'm sure she'll agree with me!

 *Kelly Morrison*

Pit Stop

Little Rascal stole my heart when I adopted him at six months old. So smart—he became my best friend, and we did everything together. So funny—while playing he would run away from me with his rear tucked in, making it look more like he was scooting! So loving—he kept me going when I lost my job and became my reason to get up each and every day. But one day God took him from me; he was on loan, and I was only blessed for a year. Though it's the hardest thing ever, I know he is waiting for me at the Rainbow Bridge where we'll be reunited forever. I love and miss you my furry, little friend and can hardly wait to see you again! -*Rose Williams*

Being first time dog owners we did quite a few things wrong. For example, our puppy ate kibble like a Hoover vacuum. Someone told us that the pup wouldn't eat so fast if we filled up her bowl and let her eat until she was full. That was a total failure, as she ate an amount more fit for a full-grown Mastiff, resulting in hourly trips outside that night.

We went through the mouthy, chewing, and impossible potty training stages, and to top it all off, Marri was a ball of pure energy. We didn't know what to do, so we took another suggestion and began fostering other dogs. Something had to wear her out because running, playing with her doggy friends, and tug were just not cutting it.

It worked! After 12 foster brothers and sisters, honing her skills in disc, and taking obedience class after obedience class, this now 53-pound Pit Bull directs her excitement towards much more constructive activities.

Marri has taught many foster dogs how to play and have a canine companion. We've also utilized her energy by taking her to the A Rotta Love Plus' breed awareness events where she has her own kissing booth (Kiss-a-Pittie for $1). She loves, kisses, and does tricks for 5- to 12-year-old kids who reside in domestic violence shelters, and she also teaches empathy and dog safety to teenage boys living in a mental health facility. Marri is a typical Pit Bull, with boundless energy and love to give, and she especially loves kids who are her same height—just perfect for giving wet, sloppy kisses right on their faces!

 *Kellie Dillner*

Mortar's story starts out sad: born at animal services, his mother euthanized, a grim outlook for him and his siblings. That is, until Rugaz Rescue took the litter of puppies, updated them on their shots, and put them up for adoption. Most found homes quickly, but skin issues and a lack of socialization caused many people to pass by Mortar and a few of his siblings. Meet-and-greets came and went, but families seemed hesitant to take on the hyper, aging puppy with sparse fur and a maniacal penchant for pulling on his leash.

Mortar was just a big ball of puppy love, always wagging his tail and ready to give kisses. It was hard to believe no one would give this beautiful boy a chance. Instead Mortar moved from foster home to foster home, with everyone hoping that someone could help calm him down. He grew handsome, but his uncontrollable energy remained. As new, younger puppies and older, calmer dogs came into the rescue, Mortar and his siblings seemed indefinitely stuck in foster care.

August came, and the rescue attended a wonderful adopt-a-thon. I went to support the rescue and as a kind of therapy to help me heal after recently losing my puppy to illness. I, too, had looked at the pictures of Mortar and decided to pass him up for a younger dog...until I met him at the event.

Though Mortar did seem hyper, he had soulful eyes which melted my heart. I wanted to take him home but was unsure if I had completely dealt with my feelings regarding the loss of my puppy. So instead of going home with me, Mortar ended up being adopted by a different family at the event.

I then became a foster volunteer for the rescue because they were so supportive during my tough time. Surprisingly, only a few days went by before I was asked to take in a dog. I was very excited to help save a life...but imagine my surprise when I found out it was Mortar! He had been returned from his new home because of his overexcitement. He looked sad when he arrived—probably confused as to why he was being moved around again. Regardless, that didn't stop Mortar from running through my house, jumping on my husband, licking the other dogs, "kissing" the kids, and chasing our cats. I suddenly understood what everyone was talking about—this dog was overflowing with energy!

After his initial "inspection" of our home, Mortar dashed around the house until he found me. He very calmly moved closer, sitting next to me on our bed. Mortar responded with kisses as I gently massaged his ears and told him what a good boy he was. The kisses were endless and he snuggled right next to me, ultimately falling asleep. I never moved him off the bed that night, and from the next morning on, Mortar never left my side. He followed me from room to room, cuddling at every chance. I knew by the next day he had filled a special spot in my heart and that he was going to stay with our family. The pup passed up by so many families (including my own) had finally found his loving forever home.

 Brianna Rodriguez

Catch-22

It was a Catch-22. We had surpassed the age of 62, which in West Hollywood means that we can own a pet, despite building and apartment owner policies which may say otherwise. However, many rescues wouldn't return our phone calls and emails because they felt we were too old to adopt a dog. I looked up dog rescue agencies online and found photos and descriptions of dogs that touched my heart. I filled out applications, answered some bizarre questions, and refused to answer others. The result was that I was ignored, told that I had to adopt two puppies, that I didn't have the energy or the time to devote to a puppy, and that I needed a house with a backyard. Apparently it's harder to adopt a puppy than a child in this city.

Undaunted, I continued my search and found a photo of "puppies." Again I wrote to say I was interested, as long as they would be about 35 pounds (the limit I thought was reasonable). And again I was sent an application that I dutifully filled out, my heart sinking. This time things were different, though. I received an email asking if I'd like to meet the puppies. Sure. This was farther than I'd ever made it in this process.

The email was followed by a phone call from a volunteer named Renee, who started with, "Hey. You're interested in adopting a Pit Bull?"

"Yikes," I replied. "I didn't know the pups were Pit Bulls."

Renee, the consummate saleswoman, backed up and told me how Pit Bulls had a bad rap and that this puppy wasn't really a Pit Bull anyway. Min Wee, as she was called, was born at Linda Blair's WorldHeart Foundation in Acton, California, an organization that saved her from euthanization. Her mother is an American Staffordshire terrier, the fancy name for a Pit Bull. Her father, as near as we can tell, is part Labrador—a passing fancy. Renee continued that the dog would definitely stay under 35 pounds and seemed just perfect for me. By the end of her pitch I was ready to adopt *Renee*! So we made a date to drive up to Acton to meet Min-Wee.

The morning of the visit Renee called to say that she might have been mistaken—perhaps the puppy was *a little* bigger than she'd told us but still just as sweet. Did we want to cancel? We didn't.

We arrived at the shelter and there was Min Wee, all legs and wearing a new pink collar. I couldn't help but note, as we stared into each other's eyes, that she probably had already passed the 35-pound limit I'd put on the dog I would adopt. But my heart had already renamed her Annabelle.

We proceeded into the get-acquainted arena, where we saw how darling she was and how nicely she played with the other dogs. We then met Annabelle's mother and sister. The sister was quite a bit smaller than Annabelle and had a sweet face. As I reached out to pet her, Annabelle jumped into my lap and stretched herself out, as if to say, "Pet whomever you want; the decision has been made."

Within three hours we were bonded to Annabelle, but more importantly, we were deemed right for Annabelle. We passed the test, despite being "elderly" apartment dwellers, and made arrangements for Annabelle to be delivered after she was spayed and vetted, which turned out to be a very long ten-day wait.

Finally, Annabelle was brought to our apartment where my husband, Gil, greeted her while I was at work. The trainer who brought her said such an emotional goodbye to Annabelle that Gil wondered if he should have left the room to give them some time alone.

When I walked in the door later that afternoon, Annabelle rushed to greet me in a frenzy of tail and belly and monster paws. "Wow," said Gil, "She didn't greet me that way." Apparently she likes the ladies.

Annabelle has been living with us for only six weeks, but it seems like she's been with us forever. She has insinuated herself into our hearts and our lives with her sweetness, her friendliness, and her intelligence. She has almost doubled in size, so my dream of owning *two* 35-pound dogs has changed into the reality of owning *one* almost-70-pound dog. Just what I wanted!

She has many friends in the neighborhood and in the building. The neighborhood friends are dogs; the building friends are people who still haven't reached the dog-friendly age of 62. She bares her belly to all of them and gets petted and tickled in return.

She sleeps in a crate and greets us effusively every morning. Now that's the way to start the day, and nobody should be deprived of it.

 *Rita and Gil Weingourt*

On Life, Love, and Friendship

This story begins in New Jersey, where my fiancée, Dawn (now my wife), prepared to relocate to California to be with me. As we loaded the car for our big excursion across country, I promised her adopted Pit Bull, Dino, I would get him a beautiful California Girl in exchange for his cooperation during the long drive.

Unfortunately Dino suffers from numerous ailments - Addison's Disease, Copper Storage Disease, Thyroid Disease, kidney stones, and steel plates in both knees reconnecting ligaments—he's our little "bubble boy." We thought another dog might be just the thing to recharge Dino, curing his lethargy, apparent sadness and depression. It was time to come through on my promise, and this is where little Lucy comes into the picture.

Lucy somehow ended up in the South Los Angeles Shelter with her time quickly ticking away. A rescue event at the La Brea Tar Pits was to be one of her last chances for adoption, but the shelter worker responsible for bringing Lucy mistakenly brought her kennelmate, Sugar. The rescue coordinator, Kelli, pleaded with the volunteer staff to go back and get Lucy. A short while later Lucy and Sugar were reunited for a day of fun at the park.

Lucy still hadn't been adopted after a long day in the hot sun, but what could have been a tragedy turned into her best opportunity for a new life when she was discovered by Linda Blair of the WorldHeart Foundation. Linda kindly agreed to take Lucy and a few others who hadn't been adopted under her wing, and suddenly their prospects were looking much better.

Linda instantly bonded with Lucy, seeing something very special in the little Pit Bull. Her beautiful, golden, marbled eyes penetrate heart and soul, but her special way of connecting doesn't just end with people—she offers her love, support, and company to other canines in need, too. Lucy instantly befriended another Pit Bull at the foundation who was unable to be around other dogs because of his aggression.

Lucy came into our lives when Dawn's brother, Tony from New Jersey (also a Pit Bull lover and rescuer), found her biography on Petfinder.com. Immediately taken in by her profile and photos, we brought Dino to visit Lucy and spent several hours talking with Linda and touring the WorldHeart facility. Linda's dedication was inspiring, and we knew we needed to do our part by giving Lucy a new home.

At home Dino and Lucy instantly became lovebirds. They spent countless hours snuggling and grooming each other, and we would frequently catch them kissing on the couch like teenagers in love. Their enjoyment of each other's company surprised us, as we never expected them to grow so close that quickly. I guess it was love at first sight.

After a while, we realized Lucy had a lot to learn. Walking on a leash, climbing stairs, and swimming at the beach (Dino's favorite pastime) were all foreign to her. Also, Lucy grew very fond of area rugs...and of tearing them up. Dino set a perfect example with his impeccable manners and willingness to lend a paw like the gentleman he is, but Lucy needed more guidance in the art of ladylike behavior. She had several quirks that needed to be ironed out, so we were in the market for an experienced dog trainer.

One afternoon Dawn and I were walking Lucy and Dino in the park, when we came across a gentleman training his Pit Bull. We stopped and watched in amazement, wondering if our dogs could ever be so well-behaved. We introduced ourselves to "Dave" and asked him numerous questions about the clicker training techniques he uses with his dog, Kai. His knowledge was vast and the deal was sealed—Dave would be our new trainer. He began working with Lucy, Dino, Dawn, and I and has helped us overcome some of our obstacles together as a team. These days Dave continues to assist us in molding Lucy and Dino into the great breed ambassadors we know they can be.

Lucy has been with us for ten months now, and it has been so much fun to see this little girl grow. From being unable to walk up the stairs to now communicating her bathroom needs by ringing a bell at the backdoor, Lucy has truly come a long way. She has even learned to crate herself during dinner time, waiting patiently for her treats (a trick we can only hope Dino will pick up on). Lucy is very affectionate and truly enjoys being a lap dog. You can find her nestled between your feet while on the computer, resting her head on your shoulder while watching TV, or snoring in your ear while sharing your pillow with you at night. She hasn't learned to swim yet, but some girls just don't like getting their hair wet. We're hoping next summer she will give it another try.

Dogs like Lucy are great for friendships—and not just their own. Linda Blair and Kelli have developed a great friendship and partnership since the La Brea event; they teamed up and have rescued numerous dogs together. As for Lucy, I can't imagine a better California Girl for Dino. She gives him friendship like no other and a new outlook on life. He now has the spirit of a young dog and loves to run, chase, and play with his sweetheart. For us, Lucy is more than a friend—she is family—and we're honored that our house is Lucy's forever home.

 Kurt and Dawn Kimmel

Invader Zim

I met Zim at the veterinary office where I was the kennel manager and studying to be a veterinary technician years ago. One of my receptionists came in with a muddy, immobile dog I thought was dead. But he wasn't dead—he was Zim.

Doc stared at the sickly-looking dog, quickly mumbled some things, and whisked him away into a run. I went back there to see Zim, who looked up at me and gave me a kiss. I then asked Doc what was going to happen, and he just gave that stern "doctor" look. I started to cry, and all he could do was look at me. I remember it as if it were today.

After we closed for the day, we bathed Mr. Zim, fed him a good meal, and set him up with lots of fluffy blankets for his skinny body to lie on. I was so excited that it seemed he would live until I got the bad news...he was heartworm positive.

Doc just glanced at me and then put his head down. He didn't want to look me in the eye, and so instead he yelled to Melissa (the vet tech), "We'll do his surgery tomorrow and set him up for heartworm treatment in 14 days." I was so relieved. I didn't know this dog and had never owned, rescued, or really even interacted with a "true" Pit Bull before, but that night I just lay with Zim and cuddled. For some reason his survival meant everything to me.

The next day I was awakened by the techs taking him for surgery. They neutered him, sewed up some wounds, and placed a contact in one of his eyes to repair a superficial corneal ulcer. Doc went the hundredth mile with this guy, who had so much wrong with him that no one in their right mind would have even given him a second look.

The poor Pittie was kept calm for 14 days and then started on heartworm treatment. It was six long months of kennel confinement, during which I shared each lunch hour in his kennel with him, until he was finally healed. God, how I loved him, but when he was finally well enough to go home, my living arrangements prohibited me from taking him. Instead he landed with a groomer and her husband. We did a meet-and-greet with their Pit Bull girl, which went very well and they took Zim home. I was completely heartbroken *and* wholly elated, knowing he was in good hands, but those hands were not mine. I could see him occasionally but that didn't change my aching feeling of loss.

I thought about Zim all the time: how he would bust my lip open by jumping in my face every morning, how we worked together every day on getting him back to health, how much I loved him and wished I could have kept him. As the years passed it got better of course, but he was always in the back of my mind.

Then one day six years after he was adopted, the groomer called: "Zim is in trouble, and if you can't take him he is going to the pound." It turned out his "parents" had divorced, and the husband kept the dogs until losing his job, which forced him into foreclosure and required him to surrender his dogs. I was shocked, and though I was at work, my friend took him in for me that very same day and sent me pictures. The dog looked too skinny—I had worked so hard on making him a chunky butt—but my Zim had truly returned!

I cried at work. Funny how things come around! I got my Zim back, and now he's not going anywhere. At 10 years old and blind in the eye that Doc tried to save, he still runs and plays and cuddles so close. Never again will we be separated. I can't imagine my life without an American Pit Bull Terrier, a life that has been so fulfilled by my Invader Zim.

 *Devlynn Saunders*

We read articles about Pit Bull abuse and fighting dog kennels, trying to understand what motivates such mindless cruelty. A letter written by Amanda Conrad took us to her "Pit Prints" webpage where we found information about rescued and rehabilitated dogs offered for adoption. The pictures and background stories made us sad and angry. We knew Pit Bulls to be intelligent, loyal dogs. Rosie, our American Staffordshire Terrier, lived with us for 16 years; she was a joy, not a problem, and more than "just a dog."

We were used to hearing the misconceptions people had: they turn on you, don't trust them around children, they're killers, there's something wrong with them. We forgave their ignorance (sort of). Now in our 50's and 60's we weren't really considering another dog but thought if we could provide a home, we should and would. There are lots of homeless Pit Bulls.

We began looking for a Pit Bull we'd be able to adopt, knowing we were too old for a puppy. Curious to learn, but unwilling to commit to a "who-knows-what" dog, we e-mailed Pit Prints for information. After qualifying to adopt, Amanda asked if we would consider a Pit Bull rescued from an extremely bad situation. The picture wasn't displayed so as not to attract the wrong people, and we were curious, though not ready to commit.

Amanda sent a picture, and he was what I envisioned a fighting dog would look like: short and muscular, weighing about 60 pounds, around four or five years old, black with stripes, one folded ear, a huge chest. He looked like the emblem on a Mack truck! He'd been starved and had heartworms. Head down, facing the camera with sad eyes, he looked like there was nothing to hope for or care about.

Surprised by my emotions, I said to my wife, "Pat, this fellow needs a chance." She looked aghast but was as sure as I that this was the right dog. We weren't going to have a "look," we were going to bring him home. So we emailed Amanda and made preparations to drive from Key West to Atlanta to get him.

When we arrived the dog lay in the grass looking away from us, disinterested and quite passive. Amanda had rehabilitated him for longer than a year before placing him in a foster home, where he stayed until we came along. We heard some of his ordeal. His entire life was alone in a cage, with no human or canine contact. When she told me he was fed once a week, I said, "Please, no more." She understood. We didn't need to bring his baggage along—he needed a new start. Amanda and his foster had done a fine job with him, he showed no adverse traits and was easy to handle.

Upon leaving, Amanda provided a black, fuzzy towel with a white paw-print on it before Pat walked him to our car. He looked back at Amanda once then lay down on his towel (still his favorite possession), not seeming to care what was next. Amanda, looking sad and hopeful, told us he was a very special little dog before turning determinedly away.

We stopped to walk him twice on the long ride home. At a truck stop a cowboy with a trailer full of horses looked and said, "Damned he's broad! Where'd you find him?" I said he was an Atlanta rescue. Looking me in the eye he continued, "Goddamn the people that fight 'em; that's a good thing you folks are doing." It made us feel good.

Hours later at a convenience store, we stopped to fill our thermos and buy snacks. The cashier watched Pat walking the dog and asked, "Is that one of them football player's dogs?"

"No ma'am, he's a Pit Bull we're bringing home from a rescue center." As I got into the car, she ran out clutching her purse. Stuffing money in my shirt pocket she said, "I'm paying for that food. Bless you folks for caring for him." Her face was damp with tears. We drove off thinking about the good people in this world.

We named him Toby, and in the morning I sat on the back steps with my arm around him. He leaned against me while I talked and started to get to know him. He seemed to understand, though he didn't make a sound—not for more than a year. Not a sound until he woofed once at someone on the porch. He was as surprised as we were and delighted with our praise. Now we're alerted to all callers.

There's so much he's had to learn. He walked off the back of my boat and sunk to the bottom of the bay. I was emptying my pockets to dive in for him when he surfaced two boats away, swimming strongly out to sea. I shouted and he came back. The only water he'd known was in his bowl, and he still avoids puddles on the sidewalk.

For months he searched behind the staircase when we went upstairs to see where we'd gone. He likes short walks near home. There's always a bacon strip for him at the diner when we go for a newspaper, and he gets hugs and biscuits from another restaurant. Everyone knows him.

A dubious newspaper editor writing about dog attacks came to see a "rehabilitated" Pit Bull. I went inside for drinks and returned to find him on the deck—my dog's head in his lap—stroking Toby and saying, "Don't worry, no one will ever hurt you again."

Walking, we were stopped by a rough-looking guy on a Harley who asked if he could pet him. We waited while he dismounted, and without hesitating he held Toby tightly and mumbled with blurry eyes, "Mine died and I needed a Pit Bull fix bad. I sure do miss her." Toby understood.

There's no issue with dogs or cats. A Cairn Terrier shares our fenced yard. Her owner regularly returns Toby's stolen bones. If the pup gets caught raiding Toby's food dish she's craftily chest butted or nose flipped out of the way.

At 2:00a.m. one morning I was awakened by a cry for help. The backdoor was open and Toby was intensely staring at a man holding a pizza box just outside the door. Wrong address? Doubtful. Inside two gates of an unlit yard? How had the door opened? I held my dog while the guy ran away. Toby hadn't barked, growled, or attacked. He just waited and stared (possibly at the pizza box).

Two years have passed and I know we weren't "just lucky." I believe if you befriend a dog there'll be a positive response. Toby's gratitude is shown with his unconditional love. He likes always to be near, and touching is even better. I'm not trying to sell something here, just trying to get across what a fine companion a Pit Bull can be. They need not be feared, only understood and loved.

 Bob Rowley

Pit Stop

Chop Chop: Junior is as hysterical as puppies can be. He pounces straight into the air, and when he lands his eyes are wide open, and he's ready to chomp on whatever made him jump. We started calling him Chop Chop, and somehow that turned into Junior Porkchop. As much as I roll my eyes at his puppy antics, he's truly brought happiness to us all! -*Holly M. Alspaugh*

A Lover, Not A Fighter: One day my daughter called me in a panic: "Mama! I saw this Pitty girl at a shelter in Boston... She needs a forever home. She needs *you*." I only knew what I'd heard about Pit Bulls, which was nothing good, but the eight-month-old pup was going to be used as a "bait" dog because she didn't have the fighting spirit...this stole my heart. At the same time, an unfortunate cat/kitten situation needed my help. Was it possible for me to foster a mother cat with her six-week-old kitten in the home of a Pit Bull? To my surprise, Fergie acted like she was their mother, sleeping and cuddling with the cats. What do I now know about Pitties? Devoted, loveable, and intelligent—I'd get another in a heartbeat. -*Gail Reed*

Nothing a Cheeseburger Can't Fix

On a Friday evening, driving home from work with my five-year-old daughter and a cheeseburger in hand, we came across a brindle Pit with a collar on running down the road. I told my daughter that we needed to turn around and try calling the owner. Being a lover of Pits, I was not worried for my safety or that of my daughter, but instead I was worried for the dog. My boss and neighbors have actually said things like, "They all just need to be shot!" and I know this is a popular sentiment. So I turned around, pulled off the side of the road, and enticed the dog with my half-eaten cheeseburger.

She came over with some hesitation and put her paws up on my door frame. When I opened my door she immediately jumped in. I tried to read her collar but it only had a vet tag for rabies, so I drove up and down the road asking several people if they knew to whom she belonged. I even stopped at a store to get the word out. My daughter and I agreed that she would have to come home with us, but what was Daddy going to say?

Well Daddy thought I was crazy, even though I told him she would just be a foster until I could reach someone. I called the vet whose phone number was on the rabies tag and found out that a young lady (a vet student) found the dog as a stray and brought her in for a rabies shot a few weeks prior. The stray had been lactating, but they found no pups.

After being unable to reach the student all weekend, I stopped by the vet office and gave them my info, stating that I would keep the dog until someone calls for her. I can't be sure, but I think the vet student may have given the dog away to someone in my neighborhood. Otherwise, how did the dog wander more than 20 miles from where she was found?

No one ever called, so I convinced my husband that our dog, Buddy (a seven-year-old, adopted Pit-mix), needed some company during the day. He bought it! Our new pup, whom we named Maddie, was so gentle and sweet-natured that we just had to keep her.

We had her spayed and her tail docked because of an injury that couldn't be easily fixed. She had some separation anxiety issues, but we taught her that her crate is a happy place. The challenge didn't upset us—wouldn't you get anxious if you had been left before?

There is nothing like coming home from a busy and stressful day and seeing my best friend with a toy in her mouth and a wiggle in her tail, just happy to see me. I'm sure glad my shadow and best snuggle buddy found my cheeseburger attractive that day. Even my neighbor, the one who suggested we shoot them, thinks my Pittie's a pretty nice girl, but we *know* she's the best!

 *Jody Robertson*

The Terrific Twosome

I remember when my husband and I decided it was time to adopt a dog. We went back and forth about whether it was fair to have one in a city apartment and if we would even have time with our busy work schedules. What about travel? We spent many weekends in Cape Cod.

Despite our hesitations, we found ourselves at the MSPCA-Angell adoption center—just to "look." But those who know me will tell you that "looking" would most definitely result in "taking home." And it did. We fell in love with a five-month-old Pit Bull. The shelter noises and boisterous other dogs vying for our attention clearly made her nervous, but when I stuck my hand in her cage, she rested her muzzle on my palm and just looked at me. I knew we had to give her a chance, so we named her Taj and she quickly became our world.

Easily adapting to our lifestyle, Taj travels with us to Cape Cod on the weekends and swims like a fish whenever given the chance. She has developed quite the personality and loves to smile at our friends. Imagine, a 65-pound Pit Bull, smiling! Smart, with enthusiasm and personality, Taj loves little kids (who, by the way, are enamored with the fact that her brindle markings make her look like a tiger). She is extremely gentle with the children who hug and kiss her, and she gives them kisses right back.

Not long after Taj's fourth birthday, I came home after work to find my husband looking at adoptable Pit Bulls online. He figured Taj needed a playmate and had found an adorable pup named Beckham, who had been left behind with his two sisters when his owners moved from their apartment in the Bronx. I agreed he was cute but was concerned that two big dogs in our city apartment would be too much.

A couple of days passed and all I could think about was Beckham's lovable face and the fact that adopting him would leave one less Pit Bull in need of a good home. So I filled out the "For the Love of the Dog" online application and waited for the rescue to contact us. The first call I received said that Beckham was already adopted, so we figured a second dog wasn't meant to be and stopped looking. Remnants of the idea still lingered in the backs of our minds, and after a few months we received another call, this time informing us that Beckham was back in foster care.

After being interviewed and our home inspected, it was time to pick up our new family member. We loved Beckham the moment we saw him, and Taj slipped right into the role of the protective older sister, teaching him the rules of the house. They now play together, sleep together, and sit side-by-side waiting for cookie time, hating the idea of being separated for even a minute (forget about walking one without the other!).

Beckham quickly began to enjoy our weekends down in Cape Cod. Who says Pit Bulls aren't water dogs? Like Taj, Beckham learned how to swim (with a little help from his sister).

Beckham and Taj are our perpetual tail-waggers, giving us *so* many kisses and so much love. My firsthand experience with Pit Bulls has been nothing but love, devotion, companionship and willingness to please. Was two too many for our city apartment? Part of me says two isn't enough!

 Heather Colleary

A Soft Spot for Oddballs

I did not know what a Pit Bull was until I already had one. When I found Zeus walking the streets, I told him to jump in the car and neither of us ever looked back at the conditions we'd come from. He is such an amazing dog that he inspired my fiancé and me to get a second Pit Bull. A former acquaintance told us he had a large litter of Pit Bulls, but when we went to his home we were horrified to find them languishing in a barbed wire cage. It broke our hearts to only take Carmella, but it was all we could really do.

Carmella turned out to be a nightmare of a puppy, but once she passed the terrible-two's, she rivaled Zeus in her own right. After Carmella we weren't planning on adding another dog, but sometimes fate directs our lives in strange ways. One day while browsing dog adoption ads for a friend, I saw a picture of a black Pit Bull puppy from a group now called Rugaz Rescue. I went to meet the puppy but was instead greeted by a gray dog running at full speed out of the foster family's home. He flipped onto his back and began spinning in the dirt, and I immediately knew "Tyler" would be mine—I have always had a soft spot for the oddballs.

When I brought him home, Zeus and Carmella weren't sure what to make of him. The first few weeks after the adoption were hard, making me wonder if I had done the right thing with regards to the dogs who were already my family. Everything worked out in the end: after a while Tyler stopped pooping in our entranceway, and months later he finally stopped running the entire length of the house while peeing.

That was a year ago. Now I couldn't imagine life without Tyler doing a cannonball into the pool every weekend, touching the ceiling every time someone comes to the front door, finding every evasive tactic to offset an anti-bark collar, or carrying a poor, unsuspecting lizard to me when he comes inside from playing.

Our family is divided for the moment while I finish law school, and my fiancé stays in our home so he's near his work. I sit in my temporary home, looking at a big, brown and white dog buried under the pillows (Zeus) and a smaller, barely visible, gray dog nestled in the corner (Tyler) of the adjacent couch. Meanwhile, my fiancé has Carmella and the newest addition, Honey, at home with him.

Despite my initial concerns and Tyler's oddball nature, adopting him was one of the best choices I ever made. Coming home to Zeus snoring and Tyler's toothy smile makes this time away from my real home so much more tolerable, and the occasional gob of drool that ends up on my arm in the middle of briefing a case comforts me.

 Jessica Rutberg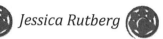

Bearing It All

I was a first-time foster mom to an abandoned Pit Bull puppy. When I found him he was severely malnourished and full of parasites, causing him to lose every hair on his little body. Even hairless and sick I could tell he was strong, so I named him Bear. For the next several months I nursed my little "bare Bear" back to health, and he finally regained the strength I knew he had in him. His beautiful brindle coat shined and his green eyes sparkled.

With good health came a new challenge: finding Bear his very own forever home. Keeping him was not an option as I already had five other pets, and my city would allow me no more. So I called several animal rescue groups, begging them to help me find Bear a safe, loving home. One rescue in Indiana was kind enough to not only post Bear's pictures and his story on their website, but they also agreed to do a background check on any family who inquired. Regardless of their support, every inquiry turned out to be agonizing. Who were these strangers asking about my Bear? Who could possibly love and care for him as I had?

Finally the rescue group called about a couple who seemed like a good match. They said there was something in Bear's green eyes that had drawn them in, and they were excited to meet him. They brought their dog Bella for the introduction, and Bear's sweet disposition had all three of them hooked. As for Bear, he just likes everybody.

So that day Bear went home with his new family and I went home to cry. What had I done? Strangers had my dog; I was worried sick and already missed him.

Later that evening, when I logged on to my computer, I was greeted by an e-mail from Bear's new parents. They said he had been playing with his new sister, Bella, since they got home, and pictures showed them curled up together on the couch. A wave of relief flooded over me.

Every couple months this wonderful couple sends updates and pictures of Bear. At first I would cry because I missed him and felt guilty about re-homing him. I had never given up a pet before and wondered if I would always worry and feel this way. These sad feelings went on until one day I received the following note:

Bear is great. He has become the perfect dog. He has mastered his walk and loves Bella to death. We play in the yard with the Frisbee and take them for walks in the woods. He LOVES car rides. He is my perfect companion.

Bear is always there to comfort me. Bella is our protector and Bear is the cuddler. He sleeps with us every night and snuggles like a person. It's great! He definitely is a mama's boy, which I'm sure he got from you, but I love it. Bear knows he is my baby.

I don't know what I'd do without him. And because of that, I have to thank you. I don't know how it happened, but I believe Bear was meant to be with me. I'm sure that is hard for you to hear because you love him so much too, but I can't explain how much he is a part of our family and how lucky we are that you were able to share him with us. Thank you again for everything.

And with that I was no longer sad for myself. Instead of just "bearing" my loss, I now rejoiced in Bear's good fortune.

 *Sandy Colacurti*

The Defender

Apollo's mother was a breeder of fighting dogs, which means Apollo was meant to fight. The owner of the stud bragged to the wrong person one day who, like a good citizen, reported him to the authorities. Animal Control came in and took the stud along with two females, one of whom was pregnant with Apollo.

Fortunately, Apollo's mother was separated from her abusive owner prior to Apollo's birth, but the fighting genes were still in her son. He came to us neutered with his ears unclipped, but he was a little feisty, which concerned us given his lineage. We soon realized we were being overly-sensitive, and he just didn't like his head being used as a basketball by his older sister, Kaida. Within a week they agreed on terms and became best friends; it's been that way ever since.

Like the Greek god, our Apollo is the patron defender of his herd and flock. He looks out for everyone in the house, especially our newest kitten, Buttons. When we first got Buttons, our older kitty, Neona, would try to bust her up a little to show that she was the boss. Each time, Apollo would run over and nudge Neona with his nose, letting her know enough is enough. It's absolutely amazing how perceptive and concerned for our safety he is.

If I ever felt for a second that my seven-year-old son, Dameon, was endangered by Apollo (or any animal for that matter), that pet would be gone. With Apollo it's been quite the opposite. I sleep well at night knowing that Apollo is sleeping below Dameon's bed. They're great friends, and we frequently find all four of our pets, including Apollo, cuddling in our son's bean bag while he plays video games.

Apollo has become a neighborhood favorite. Of course there are a few who haven't come around yet, but I believe Apollo's presence changed many people's perceptions around here about the true nature of these wonderful dogs. Apollo is a perfect example that, in the right home, even dogs who are bred to fight will show nothing but love.

 *Phillipe Gentry*

Pit Stop

Lucky Charm: Shelly was lonely so we were fortunate to rescue Lucky. He makes Shelly a perkier dog and perpetually brings fun to our lives. In the beginning when the kids would cry, Lucky would howl along with them. Every time he would see us, he would run up and bark, "Hello." He prances around the yard as if he is the king of the castle, and his newest thing is to sit along the back of the couch like a cat. Lucky is the pot at the end of the rainbow and we are *lucky* he is part of the family. *-Johnny and Christin Lockwood*

Wiggle, Waggle: Penny was wiggly and waggly—a very hyper dog with an awful habit of jumping on people. The first time I met her she jumped up to kiss me and almost knocked out my front teeth! We've nipped the jumping in the bud, and now Penny goes to work with me every day where she's made so many new friends. People say, "Is that a Pit Bull?" and I always respond, "No, that's the best dog in the whole world." I know that the other "best dog in the whole world," my Riley, is up in Doggy Heaven smiling—I think she sent Penny to me because she knew how much we needed each other. *-Vicki Castaneda*

A "Precious" Pit

About a year or so after losing our beloved Bear, a 16-year-old Pit/Lab mix, my brother and I figured it was time to seriously start looking for another dog to fill the void he had left behind. Our father had recently been diagnosed with a terminal lung condition and, as a result, the overall mood at their house was quite negative. We felt that another Pit-mix would help infuse the house with a healthy dose of positive energy. Our parents agreed and so the search began.

My brother and I had actually spent the previous year looking at Pit-mixes online, but we never seemed to connect with any of the dogs we saw...until we came across Sterling. We both fell in love with his picture instantly. He resembled a combination between a blue Pit Bull and a Weima. with beautiful amber-colored eyes, a shiny silver coat, a. dignified, handsome profile that echoed a sense of aristocra He was perfect.

It had been about 25 years since we went through a pet adoption, and we really didn't know what to expect. We contacted the rescue, the Linda Blair WorldHeart Foundation, to schedule a visit, and after several pleasant email exchanges with a terrific WorldHeart volunteer, I was told I had to be interviewed before visiting Sterling. I figured someone would call and ask a few quick, generic questions and it would be over. That proved not to be the case - the intense phone interview lasted a little more than forty-five minutes, and to top it off, it was conducted by Linda Blair herself! I was not expecting that.

Who would think that Linda Blair, a person I consider a household name, would take the time out of her busy schedule to interview me? It was a bit surreal. This nice surprise gave me some insight into the devotion Linda has for her animals.

Since Sterling is a younger dog, Linda expressed some reservation over his compatibility with my parents. She was worried that he might be a little too big and energetic for an older couple to handle. Linda's sentiments were obviously genuine and sincere, but I assured Linda that Sterling would be appropriately exercised and surrounded by love and plenty of attention. After a second phone interview, Linda finally allowed us to come and visit.

A week had passed since the second phone interview, and it was time to finally meet Sterling. My brother and I made

0-mile journey to the WorldHeart Foundation in Acton, ornia, where Linda graciously met us out front and then mptly led us on a tour of the impressive facility. We met erling and his wonderful trainer, Candie, and Linda spent he entire day getting to know us. I liked the fact that she cared so much for her animals that she took time to learn about our lives.

Linda informed us that in Sterling's previous home, the humans had attempted to make him a fighting dog. They abused him, cut into his ears, and raised him in a loveless and hostile environment. Their attempts at instilling aggression inevitably failed which was what landed him in a shelter instead of a fighting ring.

While at that shelter, Sterling somehow got lost in a bureaucratic shuffle. His quiet and calm demeanor did not bode well for him and, as a result, he went unnoticed and unfed for approximately one week. He had dropped down to an unhealthy 58 pounds when someone cleaning the back of the shelter finally noticed him. He was emaciated and weak and immediately slated to be euthanized.

Fortunately, a kind volunteer at the shelter saw some potential in Sterling and called the WorldHeart Foundation. She asked if someone would come and rescue this sweet, beautiful dog before it was too late. Linda's team generously took Sterling in, and over the next few months nursed him back to health.

My eyes well up with tears every time I think that such a beautiful creature—the most wonderful, kind, and gentle dog we have ever known—was tortured, starved, and days away from being put to sleep. My solace is that Sterling now

lives with my parents and is a healthy 85 pounds. H
chew toys, romps at the dog park, and walks along
horse trails. He gets compliments everywhere he goe.
has become quite the celebrity in the neighborhood, a
that obviously came from Linda!

Most remarkable is that since Sterling has been with
my parents, my dad's health has improved. Not that eating
well, physical therapy, and medicine haven't contributed, but
Sterling has brought so much positive energy and laughter
that his role in my father's improvement simply can't be
ignored. People hear his story and think he is a lucky dog,
but I truly feel it's the other way around. Our family owes
Linda Blair and her WorldHeart Foundation a heartfelt thank
you for a gift that can never truly be repaid. We are much
more blessed for having Sterling in our lives than he is for
having us...and that is the truth.

 The Ahmadi Family

My husband always had dogs as his best friends growing up; I did not. He was always the rescue type, who wanted people to see that the dogs considered "vicious" by many were actually the most loyal and amazing companions. So when he first suggested we rescue a Pit Bull, I was concerned! I thought of all the horrible news stories I had seen and how I wanted children one day. "Could I have a Pit Bull around a young child?" I wondered.

I was still a little hesitant when we met the available Pitties at a rescue called "For the Love of Pits." My husband was instantly great with all of them, and I started to see t many good qualities he saw in Pit Bulls as I watched them interact. We ended up with Pepper, our sweet girl, who was found by two little old ladies in a snowstorm. The instant I saw her I wanted to take her home.

At first the people in our neighborhood were skeptical of Pepper and we got a lot of stares and questions. After getting to know her, however, most of the skeptics look forward to seeing Pepper around town. Our mailman leaves her a biscuit daily, and our neighbors all come out to pet her when we walk by. People ask if Pepper can come over to play with their dogs - everyone loves Pepper the Pit Bull.

My dad, who has always had difficulty with dogs due to allergies, even adores Pepper. He takes her on walks and for car rides, and when we go out of town it's like a vacation for him to babysit her. For Christmas Pepper gets more presents than my husband and I do!

Last January we welcomed a new addition to our family: a baby girl named Gabriella. When she was born she had some breathing issues and was hospitalized several times. One time when Gabriella started breathing heavier after we gave her some medicine, Pepper ran back and forth between my husband and I as if she was saying, "Please, help Gabriella!" He was always obviously concerned for her.

People told us that when our daughter was born we would love Pepper less, but they were so wrong! Pepper is still just as much a part of our family now that she's a "big sister." I look back at the question I asked about having a child and a Pit Bull, and I can't imagine our lives without Pepper. Our daughter adores her; in fact, her very first belly laugh was tching Pepper and her dad play. Like the spice, Pepper ves our life zest, and I wouldn't give her up for anything!

 *Erin Cahill*

Early Warning Izzy

A week before Halloween I was propped up in bed with my laptop on my knees, and my adopted Pit Bull, Izzy, was stretched out at my feet. It was 10:30 at night, and I was looking forward to sleeping in the next morning. My yard and porch were completely dark, as I had turned off the outside lights before going to bed.

Izzy came into my life two months earlier from a local Pit Bull rescue organization after I saw her adorable face online. Her short, golden hair and baby-bird's-wing ears appealed to me instantly. Izzy was skinny but very energetic for a middle-aged "woman," with manners that needed a bit of polishing, but she was wonderfully friendly and non-aggressive toward people of all ages.

I was a divorcee living alone in a log-style house that faced a two-lane road without sidewalks or shoulders. There were no casual passersby in our neighborhood of newer luxury homes and one modest remaining rental, a small cracker box separated from my property by a line of red-tip trees. The current renter was a single man, a landscaper who worked long hours.

I was about to shut down my laptop for the evening when there was a thunderous *Rap! Rap! Rap!* at my front door. Alarmed, Izzy raced toward the door, barking loudly, and I picked up my cell phone from the bedside table to call 911. The police arrived within minutes and walked around the yard. Finding nothing suspicious, they did ask me if I'd seen any vehicles. One officer told me my dog had probably frightened off anyone who'd been on my porch. I might have had difficulty going to sleep that night if not for my canine early warning system.

While walking Izzy on Halloween night the next week, I noticed my landscaper neighbor through the red-tips, sitting in his yard, burning a small amount of garden debris and talking calmly to a woman on speakerphone. I returned to my house and was putting the chain on the front door when I heard a desperate person in the middle of the street, shouting, "Help me!" Again I called 911, reporting that I thought someone had been hit by a car in front of my house. Several cars stopped and a fire truck and ambulance arrived very quickly. Izzy and I sat on the porch, watching from a distance so as not to interfere with police activities.

I was stunned to hear on the news the next day that my neighbor had died at the hospital, the victim of a hit and run accident. Further stories revealed he had been struck and injured in the driveway of his home during the short time it had taken me to walk through my house after coming inside. Several days later, a state trooper came to question me about anything I might have seen. The officer told me my neighbor had lived long enough to report seeing an unfamiliar white van in his driveway a week before he was killed. On Halloween that same white van had pulled into his driveway, so my neighbor approached the driver to ask why the two men were there. The driver responded by sharply turning the van and ramming him while racing out of the driveway. Badly hurt, my neighbor had dragged himself into the street and cried for help, which is when I heard him.

The officer told me that they had not been able to locate the white van, but they suspected that at some time in the past, drugs had been sold out of the rental house. The men in the white van may have been seeking drugs and, when they realized they were at the wrong house, ran down my neighbor before he could get a close look at them.

It was a terribly disturbing episode, especially when the dead man's family arrived to gather his belongings. I couldn't help wondering if the mysterious rap on my door the week before had been the same men, looking for drugs. If my Izzy had not sounded the alarm and frightened them away, would I have been a victim instead? I may never know the answer, but I know I sleep much better with my warm friend and her no-nonsense bark at the foot of my bed.

 *Nancy Pauline Simpson*

Pitty and the Pig

When Kaos was eight years old we decided to find him a playmate. He had been the only dog in our house since he was a puppy and, being well-socialized, we knew he'd have no problem accepting another dog. Since my husband and I are Pit Bull advocates, we knew we wanted to adopt a dog of this loyal, smart, very misunderstood breed.

There are many Pit Bulls in need of rescue, but Polar, a dog we were referred to by Smilin' Pit Bull rescue, tugged at my heartstrings in a very special way. Since she was a puppy, two-year-old Polar was used by a backyard breeder in Arkansas. Bred again and again, she would sometimes go for days without food or human interaction. She was so neglected that one day, when she got her foot caught in the hog wire fence surrounding her and her puppies, she had to chew it off to detangle herself and never received veterinary care. Instead, she was put in a pen with a 400-lb. pig who became her best friend. We're told that she took care of the pig like one of her own, and she cried when they took her away from him.

In October we paid the airfare to have Polar flown to us in Ohio. Honestly, we were nervous and even started to think that maybe we should have met this dog before agreeing to adopt her. But all of those fears melted away at our first glimpse of her sweet, little face. Even though she was weak and her eyes seemed lifeless, she picked up her head to lick my husband's face. Polar was finally *home*.

After many trips to the vet and several rounds of medication, Polar was given a clean bill of health. Within weeks she had gained 20 pounds of much-needed weight and her eyes began to sparkle. Now Polar enjoys days full of sunshine and relaxation on the deck with her big brother, Kaos. She likes to play, loves peanut butter, enjoys car rides, and soaks up all the attention she can get. Every now and then we catch her snuggling with Kaos in his bed, finding comfort with him as she previously did with her puppies and her pig. It's been a long road for Polar, but now, together, as a family, we delight in each other's warmth.

 *Ron & Marlo Slusarski*

Skelly Wiggle

In all my time in working with Pit Bull rescue, I never had to drive more than a state away to pick up a dog, and I also had never adopted a dog sight unseen.

Something was just different about Skelly. She was tied in the backyard of a crack house and being used as a bait dog in a fighting pit when New Orleans animal control rescued her. Her ears had been hacked into a short crop with scissors and she was a gaunt 13.6 pounds.

When we got the call on Skeletor, the name she was given because of her gross emaciation, we really didn't know what to expect. She was tagged for euthanization and brought to the table to be helped to her death. But when the young lady went to put the needle into her, Skelly started to give her kisses. Even though she was about to die, her love shined brightly on the person taking her life. Needless to say, the woman couldn't do it.

Emaciation wasn't Skelly's only problem, but left untreated she would not have needed a needle to take her life. When I went to pick her up, she was being treated for heartworm and recovering from an emergency surgery after her uterus ruptured, too. The poor thing was so lucky to be alive!

Since our rescue had a few great Bullies needing adoption and poor, sick Skelly's chances were slim, we decided she should come live with me. After all she had been through, I knew I just couldn't let her get shuffled around anymore.

These days she still bears physical reminders of her past life: her ears, her scars all over her face and legs. Her disposition, though, is that of the happiest, friendliest, little Pit Bull you'll ever see. Her tail wags so fast when she's really happy that we call her "Skelly Wiggle." She shares her life now with not only us but also with her rescued Pit Bull brother and sister, Barry and Wonder, and her new puppy mill-rescued toy Pomeranian sister, Spicy. She is an amazing example of the true character and resilience of these dogs. After all her hurdles and hardships, her faith in us as people remains, and nothing makes her happier than lying somewhere soft, knowing that she's safe now.

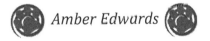 *Amber Edwards*

Pit Stop

Scary Sight: Sterling is usually very quiet and reserved, so we are alarmed one day when he starts growling at the fireplace. This goes on for a while, and so my dad gets his gun and searches the side yard, to no avail. Sterling continues to growl. Finally, my mom goes over next to him to see what's in his line of sight...and starts laughing *hysterically!* Sterling was growling at his reflection. You would think my mom's presence would comfort him, but no, now he sees her reflection and his growls escalate to wild barks! *-The Ahmadi Family*

You Can't Teach an Old Dog New Tricks, unless that dog is Aretha. She never knew the comfort of a couch or the joy of a squeaky toy until she was four years old. She was kept outside with little shelter and inadequate food and water, never feeling the warmth of a home or love of caring humans. After a VERY long haul, at the age of four, Aretha was finally introduced to all of these things that most lucky dogs learn about just after they're born. Such a happy girl and so full of soul like her namesake, Aretha not only learned to receive all the love a dog should be given, but she quickly caught on to showing her gratitude by smothering people with her kisses. *-Erin LaCombe*

When the story I'm about to tell you took place, my newlywed husband and I had been married less than a year, had adopted two dogs from local rescues in Augusta, Georgia, and were expecting our first child later that summer.

Lilly is a Lab/terrier mix (which is code for adorable mutt that's too smart for her own good), and Vegas is an American Pit Bull terrier (although professionals love to argue amongst themselves over his "true" lineage, since no one knows for sure where he came from). Vegas was dropped in the bushes in front of a very nice, elderly woman's home when he was just a puppy. She thought she had a 50/50 chance of being bitten by this unknown dog, so she named him Vegas. As he grew, it quickly became obvious that his size was going to be too much for her and her elderly mother to handle (bad hip and all), so they gave him to Heartsong Animal Rescue to find him a forever home...and that's where we found him.

One warm Georgia summer evening a couple of months after we adopted Vegas, we decided to go out for dinner. We had a huge, fenced back yard, so we thought we'd let the dogs run and play there while we were out. But just as they had served us our entrees, I received a call on my cell phone from a woman who lived up the street from us. She said she had our dogs locked in her dog pen in her backyard. Apparently they were just running around under the street lights when she came home from work, so she called to them and they came to her. She got my cell phone number off Vegas' tag and called me right away. "Just get here when you can," the woman said, "I think one of them might be bleeding somewhere. I had blood on my skirt when I went in the house. It was too dark outside to see much..."

We quickly finished our dinner and headed home to retrieve our dogs. When we got to her house, she greeted us outside and was very kind. She explained that her son had built the large kennel run in her backyard for his two dogs and that's where they stay when he comes to visit. "Lucky I could get 'em in there," she said, "Otherwise they might have wandered off pretty far." She admitted that when she saw Vegas, she wasn't sure if he would be aggressive or not, but when she called them over, much to her surprise, he was the first one to her, licking her and wiggling all over. She commented on how sweet he was and how Pit Bulls get such a bad rap. Then we thanked her for holding our dogs for us, and we took them home.

Once inside the house, no doubt exhausted by all the excitement, the dogs went and lay down, falling asleep almost immediately. Vegas was on the cool tile floor in the kitchen; Lilly by a vent in the living room. As they rested, we checked them over and saw what had happened to them in the short time we were gone. As Lilly lay sleeping, her chest rising and falling with each breath, we noticed a little glimmer of light reflecting off her ribs. Upon further inspection, we found the unthinkable: a copper bullet, used by a BB gun at close range, was lodged in her side and reflecting the light from the kitchen each time she took a breath. Horrified, we pulled out two BB's.

Vegas only had one bullet lodged in his coat, but his wounds were far more disturbing. His face was bleeding from four or five holes in his snout, where someone had shot him at close range multiple times.

I was beside myself with guilt, fear, and anger. Who could do such a thing? Lilly only had body shots because after the first hit she must have run away. Vegas, on the other hand, loves and trusts all people, so after these monsters shot him in the face, he did not turn away; he may have even gone back to them if they called him to, so they could just shoot him again.

Yet despite the fact a stranger had just shot him in the face, and he and Lilly were running for their lives, Vegas recognized the Good Samaritan and immediately, willingly let this stranger put him in a cage, somehow knowing it was for their safekeeping.

But that's Vegas. I am constantly surprised at how gentle and loving this dog is towards everybody. His enthusiasm and affection have never faltered, even when people don't give him the same courtesy. The more I researched this breed, the more educated I became as to their inherent kind nature and capacity for love. My Vegas is a shining example.

When my daughter was born Vegas paced the floors each time she cried. I think he was just as happy as we were when she started sleeping through the night! He slept under her bassinet when she slept, and if she was awake he was watching over her. Every time I, or anyone else, sat down on the couch, Vegas wanted to be next to us, touching us (preferably in our laps). There has never been a friend or a stranger that has come into our home that he did not welcome energetically with a wagging tail.

His benevolence, goofy charm, and unyielding love for humans since day one in our family have taught me that I've got no room for pre-judgment or prejudice in my life. He has also sparked the animal-loving flame within me that now burns brighter and hotter than ever before. Through his loyalty, affection, and steadfast heart he has shown me my purpose and prompted me to do all I can to help rescue, rehabilitate, and find homes for as many shelter dogs, especially Pit Bulls, as possible. I am on a mission to educate people about the joys of a Pit Bull-filled life and the fallacy of ferocious, baby-eater myths.

The happiness Vegas has brought to our family knows no bounds. My heart and mind are now open, thanks to Vegas, and I will continue to fight for Pit Bulls until the truth sets them free.

"The greatness of a nation and its moral progress can be judged by the way its animals are treated." –Ghandi

 Steffanie Prestol

It Takes a Foster

Nina was my "foster failure" (I kept her), and I hadn't had a puppy in the house since. That was nine months ago, so watching my new foster puppy, Emme, discovering the world was a real treat. Her curiosity and audacity constantly amazed me, especially because it was such a stark contrast from Nina's personality. Seeing Emme, unafraid of anything, made me wish that Nina could have had a foster home to give her the same positive early experiences.

For Nina new things, different things, or out-of-place things were scary. She was my anxious and unsure girl. Between private training sessions, a pheromone collar, anti-anxiety medications, and even a consultation with a behaviorist, Nina and I had tried everything to build her confidence and make the world a less scary place. You name it, Nina and I had probably given it a shot.

What I hadn't tried yet for Nina, though, was fostering a little puppy—and sometimes that is just what it takes. We were glad to help Emme along to a good home and happy life, but her impact on our lives was so much greater.

You had to experience Nina's irrational fears to truly understand their extent:

My boyfriend and I are on the couch watching a football game - he on one side with his laptop and me on the other with mine. Our power cords run across the ground to separate outlets on the opposite wall. Not really much of an obstacle - not unless you are Nina.

Nina begins to come into the living room and sits in front of the cord. "Unable" to cross over it, she goes around to the doorway on the other side of the room and again finds herself "blocked." She repeats the pattern of going from entrance to entrance, again and again, hoping something will give. No amount of calling her and inviting her into the room will change the fact that she "can't" cross over the cords.

When I realized what was going on, I wanted to take Nina into my arms and cry for her. I couldn't imagine living in a world where something so small and innocuous lying across the ground would be enough to keep me from one of my favorite things: cuddling my people on the couch. I also wanted to cry from frustration and disappointment. Really? After everything that Nina and I had done to help her over her fears, this was where we were? It seemed like we hadn't progressed at all. This happened about four weeks before little Emme entered our lives.

Nina immediately fell head over heels for Emme the day she walked through the door. In Nina's mind there was nothing better than getting her own puppy. In my mind, there was nothing better than Nina. If a=b=c, then there was also nothing better than a puppy for me because Emme was about to improve Nina's life.

For two weekends after taking Emme in we renovated a bathroom in the house. Tearing up old tile meant hammers and loud noises; replacing the vanity meant the new one and old one, side-by-side in the living room as we transitioned them; new tile for the floor and shower meant saws and more noises. The house was in a state of semi-chaos, full of all the things that terrified Nina.

None of it bothered Emme. In fact, she saw the construction as a whole bunch of fun. A big, empty box was something to crawl into; the loud hammering noises were an invitation to figure out where they came from; the bucket where we mixed cement and grout was a place to stick her head into and sniff. A typical puppy, Emme was curious and carefree. She had never known anything bad in the world, and for her, changes and noise just meant more adventure.

So during that time I was just as much in love with little Emme as I was with Nina because of the effect Emme had on her. With the little puppy that charged right into everything as her guide, Nina began to come out of her shell. In the middle of hammering the old tile floor, Nina made her way up the stairs to watch from the bathroom door. When the hammering stopped, Nina ventured into the bathroom to sniff it out. This was a sort of miracle to me because Nina had to weave her way around boxes, the two vanities, stacks of tile, and various tools in order to make it up the stairs and to the bathroom.

Once again I wanted to take Nina into my arms and cry. I couldn't believe it was actually my dog in the bathroom, in the midst of all of the chaos. With the help of little Emme, Nina had not just made a step forward but had instead leaped a mile. Sometimes it just takes a puppy...

 *Michelle Klatt*

Too Deep to Leap

My husband and I are firm believers in adopting dogs that might not be someone else's first choice. Usually that's a Pit Bull. After owning several Pit-mixes, we fell in love with the breed. So when we lost our beautiful, 15-year-old BJ, a sweet girl we called Beejer, we again sought a female Pit-mix as a companion for our male Pit-mix, Julius.

At the Linda Blair WorldHeart Foundation we discovered Foxy, a two-year old Pit/Sharpei mix with a bright personality. It was love at first sight for us. We're still not sure how much she loves us, but she loves her toys, her walks, her rides in the car, and my daughter's Shepherd/Boxer, Zoey.

The first night we brought her home, she hopped out of the car, ran into the house, jumped up on the sofa, jumped over the sofa, ran up the stairs, jumped on my bed, ran into the spare room onto the bed, hurtled down the stairs and outside, jumped over the hot tub, ran back into the house, jumped over the sofa, ran upstairs, jumped on my bed, ran back down the stairs, on and on and on at the speed of light. She makes an excited, high-pitched yipping sound to express her joy. My daughter promptly named her Foxy Doodle. I call her Crazy Dog.

The crazy dog episodes of deranged madness continue when she has bursts of energy, and she tears up the house in her running and jumping. Foxy has a routine that never wavers: after we take her for a walk, she goes straight to her doggy pool in the backyard, lies down, dunks her head, and gets herself thoroughly soaked before heading for a spot on the sofa. It's a mess, to say the least, so my son and I devised a plan to drain off some of her crazy-dog energy.

One evening after everyone had left our community pool, we took Foxy and Julius inside the enclosure. With youthful glee written all over her face, Foxy immediately ran full tilt toward the water, and when she was still four feet away, she launched herself into the air like a flying squirrel. Unfortunately, she didn't realize how deep the water was before diving, and she sank right to the bottom like a brick. The pool lights were on, and we could see the surprise on her face when she looked up through the water.

Foxy had the presence of mind to paddle her way to the surface, but it was clear she didn't know how to swim, so my son pulled her out and dried her off. She showed no inclination to go back in and instead went straight to her doggy pool to roll around as if to wash off the unpleasant experience.

Now we're giving her swimming lessons.

 *Sharon Noble*

Home Is Where the Dog Is

I've always had a soft spot for abused and unwanted animals (especially dogs), so when I first met Preston I couldn't keep my eyes off him. His love of life, which radiated in every move he made and *completely* masked his tormented past, left me breathless.

Rescued from a fighting operation that was using him for their own sick amusement and financial gain, Preston never received the affection he so badly craves. He won over my heart during our first introduction, and I immediately made my intentions to adopt him known. There was only one problem: my city was in the process of banning Pit Bulls, and

I would have to move so I could bring home Preston and give him the love and attention he completely deserved.

It took six grueling months until I was finally able to bring my "son" into my new residence—*our* home. During that time I would think of Preston each day, and I could almost feel him lying beside me, balled up at the end of the couch by my feet.

These days, Preston and I are inseparable, whether we're sharing breakfast eggs or car rides. We take daily walks in the park, socializing with everyone willing to give Preston a chance, all the while changing people's perception of the breed. When I leave for work, I can't help but stress over the idea that he needs me as much as I need him, and I don't like to leave him alone.

My comfort is in knowing that we have each other to get us through life's pitfalls. Even after the worst day, seeing Preston's smiling face makes my problems dissipate. We end the night cuddling on the couch and watching television, content to be together. Words can't describe the unconditional love I have for him and Preston lets me know that it's mutual. He is my everything.

We continue to train, hoping to accomplish therapy dog status so we can share the joy Preston brings to my life with others. The one who's learned the most in this relationship isn't Preston, though. He's taught me the ultimate lessons in trust, communication, and forgiveness. No matter how much he is discriminated against he doesn't discriminate back, and I am so fortunate to have such a wonderful teacher.

 *Jeff Theman*

"Until one has loved an animal, a part of one's soul remains un-awakened." -Anatole France

Going through a divorce can be an extremely lonely process; at least that's what I have always been told. The funny thing is I don't feel lonely at all. Each night I climb into my queen-size bed and focus on the soft, furry face eagerly awaiting my warm welcome; the space that could otherwise be viewed as empty is instantly replaced by a sense of wholeness. I slide into the middle and quickly pull back the comforter as a smile creeps across my face. It ly takes the pat of my hand on the mattress for the current an" in my life, my three-year-old Pit Bull-mix, Duke, to tantly cuddle up next to me.

Last night as I struggled with a terrible bout of insomnia, Duke reminded me just how loved and protected I am. After tossing and turning for a while, I had finally decided to watch a movie in the living room in hopes that I would fall back to sleep. As soon as my feet touched the floor, I heard a low, long yawn, followed by a clumsy exit from the bed and nails clicking on the bamboo floor. Duke sleepily followed me into the living room, and though I have a sectional couch where he could have easily stretched himself out, he waited until I lay down. He then took this opportunity to jump up and push himself into the curve of my knees, instantly falling back to sleep with a satisfied sigh. How could I feel the least bit alone or sad when I'm literally and figuratively surrounded by Duke's unconditional love?

This perfect little ball of joy entered my life two years ago when my then-husband had finally agreed we were ready for our first dog. I assumed we would adopt a Golden Retriever or Lab since I had grown up with them, and I obsessively scoured websites and visited the Humane Society in search of the perfect Retriever. I literally couldn't stop imagining the ideal new dog we would welcome into our home.

One day I filled out an application for a Lab-mix I saw on Petfinder.com and almost immediately received a phone call from the president of the rescue group, It's the Pits. She asked me a few questions about my lifestyle: what type of dog did I want, what was my home like, etc., and then explained the reasons she didn't think the Lab-mix was a good match. She then proceeded to tell me about a 10-month-old, white and tan Pit Bull/American Bulldog mix named Duke.

I will never forget the first time Duke sat down and stared up at me with his striking green eyes. He was an adorable puppy, yet so calm and serene. I knew I had found our dog, and from the moment he entered our home, he touched me down to the deepest reaches of my heart. Cesar Milan says, "You don't get the dog you want, you get the dog you need," which has always resonated with me about Duke, who has proven to be that and so much more. He is truly a gentle soul but can also be strong and a bit stubborn. He has forced me to show a stronger side of myself as the "pack leader," a side I didn't even know I had.

Duke makes me laugh and smile on a daily basis, and I never get tired of watching him bound across the yard after a ball and pounce on it as if it were the most exciting thing he has ever done. But his persistence makes me laugh the hardest. For example, whether I'm reading for enjoyment or working on my laptop, Duke will try and get me to play with him by bringing me a toy and nudging under my book (or laptop). Telling him "no" simply sends him on a silent stroll back to the toy box to give it a try with a different toy. This goes on again and again and each time he silently, patiently waits to see which toy will finally win me over. Of course he wears me down, and I can't help but laugh and take a break from my task to indulge him.

Duke is, simply put, the sweetest dog I have ever known. And, although I may be biased, he attracts strangers wherever we go. At first they are drawn to him because of his appearance, but as they look closer, it's his gentleness that really makes people smile. He sits with me at coffee shops, quietly watching the world go by and providing entertainment for small children. Parents are always good to ask if he's friendly, and then their children are delighted by his soft and tender kisses (which he's happy to dispense, even after a good ear pulling!).

Above all I love Duke for his kind heart, unconditional love, and mellow nature. I am forever grateful to Beth Gruff and It's the Pits for saving his life and perhaps even mine in the process. They have certainly given me a priceless gift which I never grow tired of or take for granted. I am lucky and blessed to have this spectacular animal in my life and, of course, in my bed.

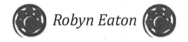 *Robyn Eaton*

Turn the Radio Up: Among her many otherwonderfultraits, Juno is a goofball. She can enjoy an old hair scrunchie for days without getting bored, and I delight in seeing her play head-butts with my other pets, including the cats! Juno loves listening to any kind

of music, and her new thing is to turn on the radio. Her play style mirrors the tempo of the song: if it's got a fast beat, her play is very hyper; if it's a slow tune, she lays her head on my lap or chews on a toy. She whines to the radio during pauses between songs, eager to hear what's coming on next for another round of good fun. -*Marva Burnette*

Discrimination Is a Pittie

After losing my beloved Copper, rescued 14 years ago, I doubted any dog would or could ever fill the void she left. See, Copper and I had moved to Ohio a few years back, when we noticed "we were not in Wisconsin anymore." The laws, the people, and the news appeared to all be against the loving Pit Bull breed. We didn't understand it and felt like outcasts, which was very difficult. So although it had been about eight months since Copper passed away in my hands from melamine poisoning, I wondered if I wanted to endure the things that go with owning a Pittie again.

Day after day I came home from work, and there was no little head peeking over the door to welcome me. Life without a dog was too much to bear, so we visited a rescue and were shown several very nice Pit Bulls and mixes in different sizes and colors. We spent time with each but knew we found the one when we were introduced to a sweet, one-year-old brindle gal called Dory that my husband thought was a rare and exotic color. I saw a gentle heart and soft eyes as she quietly examined us amidst hundreds of barking, bouncing dogs. Dory was content just to have her head petted, paying no mind to the chaos around her. This was *her* time to shine, and she did.

We snuggled on a blanket in the grass, and Dory wanted nothing of the treats or toys we offered her. Instead she simply enjoyed our attention. We thought about her on the trip home, and I drove up alone the next day to make sure our feelings were true. This time Dory looked me in the eyes, telling me, "It's time to take me home." So spayed, micro-chipped, and vetted, she finally came home, a trip which proved challenging because she was afraid of cars and suffered severe car sickness (something we would have to work on).

Dory was renamed "Corra," after the holocaust survivor and author, Corrie ten Boom. She potty trained fast and slept in the crate at night. We immediately noticed a joyful skip in her gait every time she passed another dog on our walks, so we went back to the rescue to find her a playmate. I was drawn to a wary fawn called "Joey," who was very different from Corra and known to be afraid of men. Well, he wasn't afraid of my husband—he curled right up to him and asked for a belly rub.

Corra's severe car sickness kept her from joining us on our trip to the rescue, so she had to wait to meet Joey, now Toni, until we brought him home. Ever wonder what happens when two very submissive dogs meet? It's hilarious. Corra walked up and plopped under Toni's feet while Toni gave her kisses all over her face—they were a perfect match.

For the first six months, Corra and Toni stuck to me like glue. Seeing as both dogs had been left in yards without food, water, or shelter, their clinginess was understandable. American Staffordshire Terriers, in general, are known for being kind, loyal, and loving, but the amount of love and devotion they have to give is something you must experience to comprehend. I was glad to experience it all over again with Corra and Toni, who are completely fulfilled by our touch and attention. They are shadow dogs: if I'm in the kitchen, they are there behind me lying down; when on the computer, they are on the couch behind my desk or at my feet; if we are walking on my folks' large open farm field, they never go further than twenty feet before looking where I am and running back to me. It breaks my heart to know my dogs, who are the perfect companions, were tied out in yards alone, left to suffer in isolation during their previous lives.

People say such bad things about Pit Bulls, but I can tell you that Corra and Toni were two of the three dogs out of seventeen who aced their general obedience test. They did the "long down" command across from the cat adoption door—how's that for pressure? Although they have toys in a basket on the floor, they won't play with them unless I take them out, asking permission for nearly every want and need. I surmise that rescued dogs know how bad life can be because they've already lived it, so they do all they can to avoid ending up alone and empty again.

Despite all the prejudice we endure on behalf of our dogs, we love having them in our home and walking and playing with them. A life without the comfort of a Pittie, why bother?

 *Susan Cavote*

An Easter Surprise

I jokingly refer to my house as the "Black Dog Lodge." I have a soft spot for black dogs because they so often get overlooked in shelters. It's referred to as "Black Dog Syndrome."

My newest foster, Miss Ella, is a beautiful, big-eared, black Pit Bull whom A Rotta Love Plus (ARLP—a Rottweiler and Pit Bull rescue in Minnesota) chose just for me. The day Ella arrived at my house she was a skinny, stinky little girl with a big head and an even bigger heart. As her body caught up with the rest of her, she quickly adapted to life with my two Black Labs, easily inserting herself into the family.

Easter weekend we all went for a walk, and Ella decided she wanted to go on an Easter egg hunt (as per the season). She found a "surprise" under a car, which I thought would be a dead, decaying squirrel. But as I approached, I realized that instead she'd found a puppy—yes, a puppy! I quickly took the dogs home and went back for Ella's pup. The little guy was so scared he wouldn't come out, so I sat across the street and talked to him for about 20 minutes. The neighbors must have thought me nuts to be sitting on the curb, talking to a car, but my patience paid off. He finally came out, and I scooped him up and carried him home. After many days of searching, I finally located the "guardian," who agreed Gus (as I named him) was better off with me. ARLP welcomed him into the rescue group, even though it was highly doubtful Gus had much, if any, Pit in him.

Ella, of course, was the happiest dog ever and so proud of her find. She bonded with Gus, and they became the best of friends—or twin terrors depending on the day. Miss Ella considered Gus her very own, best, most fun toy ever! She doted on "The Guster" and he reciprocated her love. Ella and Gus romped and played, then fell over with exhaustion together on the couch, only to start playing again minutes later. Gus was with us for two months before ARLP found him the perfect home.

If you are worrying about Miss Ella losing her "toy," there is no need for concern. I'm still her toy - she adopted me! Ella is pure joy embodied in a compact, 50-pound, Pittie body. She is currently in obedience class, learning the skills she needs to pass the Canine Good Citizen test and serve as a positive Pittie role model.

It all worked out in the end. I look forward to sharing my home with another foster dog soon, and Miss Ella is always on the lookout for a new toy!

 *Marie Morzenti*

I had been searching for months for the perfect Pit Bull puppy to add to our pack, first visiting Best Friends Animal Society in Kanab, Utah, and then monitoring Petfinder. com. One day I found myself continuously returning to a photo of a dog with a sweet, black and white face. I went to bed that night thinking of her and awoke the next morning with the dog still on my mind. It seemed that the time had come to contact the rescue and fill out an application.

I learned from the rescue that Arial, now Emma, was born without one of her front legs. She was surrendered to a shelter in Baltimore, Maryland, due to this "medical condition" when she was only five weeks old. How sad and short-sighted of the people who dumped her—to us she was simply perfect; her missing leg only adding to her amazing character and wonderful personality. It took a month before we were able to bring her home, but about four months after beginning my search, I picked her up from the veterinarian's office who had conducted her spay, and Emma finally joined our family. She was an absolute angel from that first day—sweet, gentle, and very calm—amazing for a seven-month-old puppy.

About three days after we brought Emma home, she began growling at us when we petted her on her right, rear leg. I noticed a black mark through her white fur and thought that maybe someone had kicked and bruised her. When it seemed to get worse, I took her to my veterinarian, who shaved the area to reveal a necrotic wound. The vet thought Emma had suffered tissue damage from her surgery that could have been caused by a variety of things. In the end we learned that it was a thermal burn caused by the previous vet placing a heating pad on Emma when it was too hot. Now she has a large pink scar with no fur on it, but I think it just adds to her enormous character.

When people first meet Emma they often feel sorry for her. I constantly hear, "Oh, God bless her, she's missing a leg." Dogs, unlike humans, do not dwell on their handicaps or let it slow them down. Emma runs faster than some of her pals, jumps up and down steps, and loves to fetch toys and play tuggie with her four-legged friends. One of her many nicknames is "Roo" because she hops like a kangaroo to get up the steps or onto the sofa.

Pit Bulls are one of my favorite breeds because of their intelligence, devotion, and sweet, loving dispositions, and

Emma is the epitome of all these fantastic qualities. Just by being herself she teaches people how misunderstood Pit Bulls are. She's the perfect companion and family pet—a delightful girl who brightens the day of everyone she encounters. The way people so easily fall in love with her, and how her presence in my life has made me a better person, make it difficult to decide whether she's Cupid or an angel—either way, all she is missing are wings and a halo—this dog is truly divine!

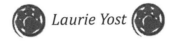 *Laurie Yost*

Sheera Unchained

From the age of five I was the child that brought home every stray in the neighborhood, fed the alley cats, and spent my free time volunteering at the local animal shelter or standing in a picket line outside the dog track. Luckily, I had understanding parents who supported me, my pets, and my projects. The animals all touched my heart as they lived out their days at our home being spoiled and given unconditional love. But none of them touched me as deeply as Sheera has.

I met Sheera through a chain link fence while visiting a friend's house. She was tied to a tree in the neighbor's yard with only two feet of freedom. She didn't have a dog house or bed, and there were no food or water bowls. Beaten, helpless, and scared with her skin hanging from her bony structure, her predicament broke my heart.

For two long weeks I watched her and talked to her through that fence. She would stand and shiver from the cold as the snow covered the ground. Over time we became friends, and she would wag her tail at the sight of me. Because of the fence I couldn't touch her or get close to her, but I had grown attached and wanted to save her life. Her current state of suffering just didn't seem fair.

I called the SPCA on a daily basis to report her terrible environment. Their representatives visited the house numerous times and were able to at least give her the shots she needed. After many visits the SPCA finally gave the owners 10 days to provide adequate living conditions or else they would confiscate the *animal*. This was not good news because many shelters don't adopt out Pit Bulls. They are instead typically euthanized upon arrival, and the idea of this broke my heart. As I saw it, her life was about to end suddenly and I was the one who signed her death warrant.

With thoughts of her keeping me preoccupied all day and most of the night, I finally decided to do something drastic. I gathered my courage, along with my checkbook, and knocked on the owner's door. As anticipated, they didn't have any problem parting with their pet...for the right price. It should have been immediate ecstasy—I mean I just saved a dog, right? Instead, I walked into their backyard to collect my new dog and was overcome suddenly with fear. This was a Pit Bull: a supposedly mean and vicious breed which I knew nothing about. I had never touched my new dog or even been within six feet of her, but with my jaw tightly clenched, I reached down to pet her head. To my surprise, she jumped up on me and licked me from chin to forehead! Turns out she was vicious...a very vicious kisser with an extremely wet tongue! It seemed like she knew I was there to take care of her, to rescue her.

For the first time I, myself (not my parents), was the proud owner of a very sick and emaciated Pit Bull. She was broken and ill, but I didn't care because I loved her and she needed me. Three days after I rescued Sheera, I had outpatient surgery done on my left knee. She lay with me on the couch all week, watching soap operas and dozing. She had been starved, kicked, hit, and imprisoned by humans, yet she trusted me without question. I was blown away at how loyal she was to me right from the start, staying by my side and following me everywhere. We were instant friends and companions. I knew I was meant to have Sheera in my life as though we were kindred spirits, destined to teach and love each other.

As the guardian of a Pit Bull, I now know personally the public scrutiny these dogs receive: at Petsmart, at the park, walking in my neighborhood—the sharp stares and obvious avoidance. I want to show everyone all of Sheera's scars, explain to them the life she has survived, and make clear that everyone deserves better. I want them to know the Sheera I know, the one who cuddles up with me at night and makes me feel safe when I am alone, but I often smile politely and walk away because there is nothing I can say to change peoples' minds. With Pitties it often takes bringing one into your home, experiencing their love for yourself, and allowing it to change your life. Words just don't work with most people.

I think Sheera knows this too, for when she meets new people she stands shyly and wags her tail, hoping that they will give her a little love. Every now and then someone stops and lets Sheera kiss them (her favorite thing to do to new people). They are people like me with a Sheera at home, people who understand that it's not the breed.

In the six years since I marched into a stranger's house and demanded they sell me their pet, my life has completely changed. Sheera gave me the courage to fight for what I believe in, and she has brought me the greatest joy. She is a healthy and happy dog with scars from her past life that are now barely visible, but they are scars I will never forget. She is still very sensitive to the cold and will avoid touching the snow, which tells me that she remembers it, too. Sheera spends most of her days napping on the couch, playing in our backyard with her Boxer brother, or letting my two-year-old daughter crawl on her and pull her ears.

I didn't know a thing about Pit Bulls when I became Sheera's guardian, but I know now that the horror stories and bad rap are completely false. She is the best dog I have ever owned, and I've owned a lot. She has changed my views and Pits will forever be my favorite breed. Much like children, dogs just need unconditional love and gentle guidance. And like children, they are a direct result of their environment.

 *Kristin Kestler Turner*

How One Saved Many

We were building our first house and I wanted a dog —a dog who would love us and whom we would love—a companion. We never imagined that Grace would provide us with so much more.

The early part of this gorgeous girl's life was filled with generally unforgivable abuse and neglect, untreated illness, and unfathomable loneliness. After being found running loose and then cooped up in a garage for a while, she spent a year and half at a boarding kennel occupying the first indoor/outdoor run, which is where we met her. On the days of our visits, we would pull up to the kennel and see her staring longingly at the cars in the parking lot. She was always still, appearing at first glance as a statue: standing on all fours equally, neck stretched out, head parallel to the ground but as high as her neck would reach, ears back, eyes open wide.

We would get out of the car and turn to approach the kennel office. Without fail, our first steps would cause Grace's ears to shoot straight up into the air. She would remain still, focusing intently on us. Immediately upon making eye-contact, Grace would turn and, at the speed of light, dash through the seemingly small doggy door to the interior kennel. How she knew it was us, we'll never know—but she knew.

Neither my husband nor I fell in love with Grace at first sight, but we could not leave her where she was. From the day she entered our home, Grace was my shadow. She cuddled as close as she could when I lay on the couch, was my co-pilot when I ran errands, and never hesitated when I asked her to do something. Little did we know we had adopted our perfect dog—so grateful for our love, returning it unconditionally.

Grace accepted every stranger and made each individual in her presence feel like the most important person in the world. She never held grudges for past experiences, and without question she loved everyone she encountered; it was a love you could feel deep inside. What I most admired about Grace was her ability to live each day to the fullest, her amazing spirit glowing in everything she did.

Despite not falling in love with my Gracie Lou Mae at first sight, I now ache with every moment I live without her. Though a heart tumor took her from us too soon, Grace's memory lives on through "For the Love of Pits," a Cleveland-based Pit Bull dog rescue. Solely because of Grace, the rescue was formed, and so many Pit Bull dogs' lives have been saved. In each dog we rescue, we see a little of our Gracie Lou Mae: our first Pit Bull dog, our special girl, our heart.

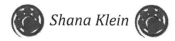 *Shana Klein*

A devastating loss shattered me beyond words; starting each day was a struggle and I didn't know what to do or where to turn. Then one day fate led me to Petfinder.com. This was my first brush with the website and I was stunned by all the rescue groups longing to find a foster family to temporarily take in a dog, to love and care for it until a forever home could be found. Or better yet, to adopt. In the midst of all those faces staring at me—puppies, young dogs, and adults—there she was, my Libby, a 10-year-old Pit Bull listed by Hot Water Rescue of New England.

Libby, a gentle old soul, came from a local pound. Not a shelter where she had better odds of being adopted but a pound where dogs' fates are usually sealed as they walk through the door. Being a "senior," which no one seems to want, Libby was especially imperiled. After two months of living at the pound without *any* inquiries, Hot Water stepped in to give her a chance.

Libby spent most of her years as a backyard breeder, tied to a drain spout with only a piece of plywood for "shelter" from the elements. I suppose she felt lucky when she was finally moved into the basement. Was it because it was too cold outside? Or was it the neighborhood complaints to Animal Control that made her abusers "hide" her where the neighbors could no longer see her suffering? Whether Libby eventually escaped or was tossed out because she could no longer breed, the important thing is that it was the first step on her road to freedom.

The first time I saw Libby I had no idea what to expect. She walked up to me, tail wagging, and we greeted each other with kisses. She had hair loss on parts of her, and had indentations around her neck from years of being collared and chained. She didn't even look back when I walked her to the car with no leash. She just jumped inside, knowing she was on her way home. I named her "Libby" because she had been liberated and "Rose" because I don't think anyone ever thought she was beautiful until that day.

That first night at home Libby slept at the bottom of our bed on top of her own blanket. Never before knowing this comfort and warmth, it was the best thing I had to give her, and to this day that's her place. Because she had been chained outside most of her life, Libby never went into the yard alone for fear of being left out there. I stood with her while she did her business in the pouring rain and watched as she quickly rushed back inside, afraid the door would close behind her if she lingered too long. Even now she is somewhat hesitant, always looking for me to be there—and I am.

Libby doesn't know the chain of events that occurred because of her, but she has been my inspiration. I have become a strong advocate for the breed and have gone on to foster other Pit Bulls for Hot Water Rescue, loving and caring for them until they find their forever homes. With each one I save there is room for another, then another. Libby has a little brother now, too: another Pit Bull I adopted just hours before his time had ticked away at the pound.

My message to Libby: *"Libby, I can't give you back all those years. I can't take away those days and nights when you were left alone in cold rain, feeling the weight of a chain around you. I can't give you back all those times you didn't feel the warmth from lying by a fire with a loving family around you, or a ball being tossed to you. I can only give you what it should have been and what it will be. I don't know how long you'll be with us; it doesn't matter.*

And when the day comes for you to cross over the Rainbow Bridge, I'll be right beside you. But just know that because of you, others have been rescued and have gone on to loving forever homes. Even your little brother is here because of you. Just know that your life is worth something; it does have meaning. And that day, Libby, when we first met, I realized that angels come in all forms. That special day, Libby, when we rescued each other."

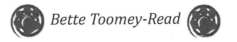 *Bette Toomey-Read*

Pit Stop

Frank the Tank is one lucky dog. He went from wandering a store parking lot at five months old, to being fostered by a woman with 20 other dogs (can you say "playtime!"), to finally being doted on by my mom and me for the rest of his life. A life which, by the way, is filled with dog parks, daily massage, ball play, swimming, wonderful plastic bottles to crush and pounce on, and role playing the life of a toy Poodle lap dog. Frank even gets to serve as "reindeer" for neighborhood rollerbladers on occasion. My friends wish they could be Frank, and honestly, so do I! *-Judie Stork*

Time Will Tell: Java was in such bad shape when I met him at New Hope Pit Bull Rescue that my in-laws didn't even want to get out of the truck. He looked beaten-down, was mangy and full of greasy scabs, and emitted the worst odor imaginable. He was such a mess that we couldn't even tell what color he was! But when he started kissing me and wagging his tail I knew there was hope, and since we took him home eleven months ago he's turned into the most loving, sweet, obedient, funny, silly, excitable friend I have ever had. His fur has finally grown back in, and it turns out he's a beautiful, chocolate Pit Bull! *-Bonnie Ellefson*

Pit Bulls are ugly. Pit Bulls are vicious. Pit Bulls kill people.
I wouldn't want to go near a Pit Bull.

These and similar statements are what you often hear when you tell people you have Pit Bull. Or, people who obviously find your dog charming shy away when you tell them it's a Pit Bull.

Had you asked me my opinion of a Pit Bull two years ago, you may have heard the aforementioned statements come out of my mouth. I may have shied away. But it all changed for me the day I met Joanic and her gang of 15+ Pit Bulls from the Buster Foundation.

I always wanted a big dog and was a St. Bernard-kinda-gal. My first dog was a Saint with health and psychological issues. Still, I loved that dog during his entire, tragic, two-year life. It took me another two years to feel ready for a new dog and, of course, I looked for another St. Bernard. I came across a Tosa Inu (Japanese Mastiff) named Xena on petfinder.com, who was very big and St. Bernard-like. So I contacted the Buster Foundation to meet her, only to find out that someone had already applied. But Joanie, the director, told me the Buster Foundation was a Pit Bull rescue and she had some pretty amazing dogs who might be a perfect fit.

Although I'd read about Pit Bulls before, I hadn't ever thought of adopting one. I looked at all the dogs on Joanie's website, found two I liked, and ironically, they were the same two Joanie thought might be a good match. The next step was for my friend, Frank, and I to head over to Joanie's house to meet them.

Those dogs, simply put, immediately smashed all our preconceived notions about Pit Bulls. They were all over us, so friendly and loving, listening to our every word as if desperately trying to convince us they would be the best companions ever. Their antics were endlessly amusing, like the way their whole bodies wagged instead of just their tails. They didn't just run around the backyard, they looked like little rockets; and instead of just listening to our commands, they competed to see who could appease us faster. Considering all that these dogs had been through in their lives, their openness to humans and sweet dispositions amazed us.

The decision was tough but we decided to adopt Lydia (Liddy), and a week later Joanie brought her to our home. Liddy really couldn't be nicer, and it only takes a few minutes with her to fall in love. Her best friends are two Yellow Labs, and she delights in removing squeakers from toys and pulverizing tennis balls.

There are still people who give us a hard time with their media-fed opinions about Pit Bulls, but our Liddy was voted the Valentine's Day photo contest international winner. Can they say the same about their dog? Her kindness makes her a "poster Pit Bull" (not just our opinion).

Our Valentine Queen may be a thief of hearts, but she's certainly nothing like the things you may have been led to believe about the breed. Like any good queen, she's nice to her people and always seems keen to please.

 Beatrice Boehme

From "Criminal" to "Caregiver"

Callie is a Pit Bull rescued from death row. I received information about her in a rescue email the evening before she was to be killed JUST for being a Pit Bull in an area of the country where they are frequently bred to fight. Her picture came up with sweet, Pit Bull-looking eyes, and it said she was an American Bulldog. I knew nothing about Bulldogs but sent her picture to a friend, who was very interested but couldn't get the go-ahead from her husband that same evening. I had heard how sweet Callie's disposition was and so I asked my rescue contact to send her to a vet who could safely board her until I could get down to South Carolina (from my home in North Carolina) three days later.

As busy as the rescuer was, she sent me a few vet offices to contact in her area. I picked one and a volunteer drove Callie to safety. My intent was to foster her until my friend could adopt her, and if she couldn't take her I would find her another "furever" home. At least she would get to live.

I picked Callie up from the Hartsville Veterinary Clinic, where she had received a microchip, rabies shot, and treatment for all her worms. Thankfully she was heartworm negative, but she did have mange, and her spay revealed that she had been pregnant. This sweet girl had been picked up by Animal Control when a man complained that she and a Beagle were eating out of his trash. So from life as a stray eating garbage, Callie came north to my house where she was treated like a queen!

My friend ended up not being able to take Callie, and though I've been involved with rescue for years, I wasn't used to such a strong dog with a low center of gravity, and I needed to quickly teach Callie about acceptable behavior (in and out of the house). My friend, John, a lawyer in NYC who rescues and trains Pit Bulls, graciously answered my daily emails regarding my newfound challenge. I wasn't sure I could manage this big, strong dog, my first Pit Bull, but I followed John's advice and started training her with frequent sits on our walks and plenty of rewards for good behavior while playing. Callie learned very fast; I was amazed at how smart she was and how much she wanted to please me.

Soon I found Amanda at Paws4Ever in Mebane, NC, a Pit Bull advocate and trainer/rescuer. I enrolled Callie in

Amanda's Pit Bull manners class to further her training and, somewhere along the way, we fell so in love with Callie we couldn't let her go. My son wanted her to be his dog when he got a house in a few years. I said okay, but as I knelt into her crate in my bedroom each night, kissing her head and promising her she would always be safe, I wondered if I really could ever let him take her.

At night she snuggled up with her blankies, sighed, and fell into her deep Pit Bull sleep. In the mornings she would bring her pink blanky out of her crate in her teeth, prancing about, showing it to me and the other dogs, not dropping it until breakfast was served. My Lab and Callie would take turns holding each other's Nylabones for the other one to chew, and they delighted in each other's company. Callie learned how to play nicely with all dogs (big and small).

Next, she took a Canine Good Citizen class at Paws. She failed the exam because she was too interested in the "stranger with a friendly dog." She then took pre-agility, did well, but wasn't hyper enough to really excel at or even enjoy it. The pre-agility training gave her the boost she needed to then go back and pass the Canine Good Citizen exam with flying colors, giving me hope that she could someday get registered as a therapy dog—her mellow personality made her perfect for the task.

I bought her a red service dog vest, sewing the CGC patch on one side and an, "Ask to pet me, I'm friendly," patch on the other. When we go out in public she wears the vest as a Pit Bull ambassador to the world. She and I teach responsible dog/

Pit Bull ownership, emphasizing the importance of spaying and neutering, training, and having a dog live indoors as a precious family member.

Callie brings so much joy to everyone we meet - elderly people and toddlers, too—who receive plenty of licks in exchange for hugs around her big, strong neck. People often say to me, "I didn't know a Pit Bull could be such a nice dog. I thought they were all killers!"

As a nurse practitioner in cardiology, I know the benefits patients derive from therapy dogs well. In the fall Callie will start her therapy dog training at Paws4Ever in Mebane, NC. Callie's loving, even, thoughtful temperament makes her the perfect therapy dog. She still has a crate in my room, but I often wake at 3a.m. to find her snuggled up in my arms with her head on my shoulder or chest. This dog is a precious jewel. She has brought me, my family, and other dogs so much joy and love, and I cannot imagine life without her now. Callie is proof of what great dogs Pit Bulls can be and how important responsible dog ownership is for ANY breed of dog.

 Cathy Nakayama

Clear Vision

This morning as I rub my sleepy eyes and stretch my arms across the bed, I notice Tommy and Blossom cuddled up on either side of my legs. Blossom lies on my left, her head resting between her paws, her cute face puppy-like, her eyes peacefully closed, her tiny white muzzle surrounded by shiny black fur. Tommy is under the covers against my right side, and I look over and see my husband, also peacefully beside me. What a way to start the day! The dogs are blessings to us, and it is a joy to be their caretakers and shepherds.

Tommy and Blossom are best friends; they sleep side-by-side, play for hours with the same toy, lick each other's ears, and put their noses together in an affectionate way. You would never know that when bony, malnourished Blossom was six months old she was found tied to a vet office's mailbox just off a highway. Or that she suffered from mange and had to have surgery for eyelids that grew inside out.

We adopted Tommy through Paw Prints Rescue. Found stranded in the streets when he was only a few months old, he was malnourished and afraid of certain hand gestures and common household tools. We loved on Tommy every day while socializing him with other dogs and people to create a safe home for him. At night he cuddled up to me like an infant in a mother's arms (and still does). It was almost like he had never experienced true, unconditional love before and was soaking it all up in my arms. His little head (now big head!) rested in the nook between my shoulder and jaw line. His tiny nose rested on my neck, and the tender smile on his face while he slept made my heart feel complete.

Spence and I have a tremendous love for the breed, and we believe others would, too, if they were properly educated about Pit Bulls. The media slanders these innocent creatures, improperly identified as bad dogs when they are truly victims of irresponsible pet ownership. They always fail to show folks like us who have socialized and rehabilitated our dogs to be upstanding members of society. Though it breaks our hearts, the only thing we can do is to set an example as responsible owners and hope others see Tommy and Blossom in a different light than what is on the 5:00 news.

 *Jennifer and Spence Kile*

Rudy the Runt

My granddaughter had told me several times about her stepbrother bringing home two Pit Bull dogs, one of whom was pregnant. Rudy (the runt) turned out to be only a third the size of the other puppies, and he struggled with nursing and walking, sleeping most of the time. Upon visiting the eight-week-old pups, my heart went out to little Rudy because his legs constantly slid out from under him, and getting around was quite the chore.

I took Rudy to my vet to determine his chances for survival. She said he seemed to have neurological damage and couldn't really predict his future. Feeling a strong need to nurture him, I took him home and introduced him to my two Chihuahuas, Co-Seta and Loopy. They weren't too taken with Rudy but we kept him anyway.

I have hardwood floors and tried everything to make it easier for Rudy to get around—finally settling on rubber mats. Rudy became stronger as time went on and now gets around pretty well. His legs still go out from under him on slippery surfaces but Rudy is a love. For the past two years we've played it by ear like the vet suggested, giving him the best quality of life possible. Rudy's favorite thing is to tease his Chihuahua sisters by pulling their blankets out of their beds (which we smile about even though it makes Co-Seta and Loopy so mad).

I would have missed so much fun if I hadn't given Rudy a chance. Despite his few health problems, he's the best! The most unique thing about him is his gait. He throws his legs out in a very stiff manner and looks just like a Tennessee Walking Horse. This, along with his personality, gets him so much attention. Rudy may be the runt and have seen his share of challenges, but like the primary-colored rubber mats strewn about my house for him, he's brightened my life.

 Linda Beals

Remixing Remi

About four years ago I decided to adopt a dog. It hadn't been long since Spot (our family friend of 13 years) had passed, and I was eager to fill the gap missing in our home. I found a local rescue group called "For Our Friends" through Petfinder.com, and Dharma, a one-year-old American Staffordshire Terrier, became our new mascot. She was hyper and easy to fall in love with...but there was still something missing.

It wasn't until six months later that I realized Dharma needed a friend. I had been volunteering with For Our Friends and knew of a male Am Staff who needed a home. Bentley (as he was originally named) had been dumped by a man on Long Island. He had some signs of neglect, including obesity and improperly cut and infected dew claws. The true sign of abuse, however, came to light when I brought him home. Remix (as we now call him) snapped at everything that came near him. No one could walk him because he would lunge, growl, and bare his teeth at whoever we passed on the street.

It was terrible. The last thing I wanted was for him to confirm his breed's bad rap, but research, patience, and practice revealed that Remi was not inherently mean—he was just downright scared. Once I realized his crazy behavior was a result of his fear, coupled with the instinct to protect his family, I began working to change his behavior. I started a calming ritual by saying, "Remi, it's okay," in a soft voice. When he regained his composure, I would reward him with affection as I repeated the mantra. He would sometimes fall asleep to this.

Back in control, I started walking Remi again, this time without Dharma. Any time he would growl at people, I would quickly start the mantra, "Remi, it's okay." It had to be done well in advance, as soon as people were within sight. If his hair stayed raised through the mantra, I would hold him down lightly by the neck as dogs do to one another. It seemed to remove the burden of having to protect me and reminded him that I had the situation under control.

With time (four months) and dedication to the process, Remi has become a model citizen! We walk him on a loose leash now and have no trouble when people approach. Remi was an extreme case, proving that any dog can change with patience and persistence by those caring for him.

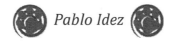 *Pablo Idez*

Pit Stop

The Long Cobblestone Road: When Jaydee came into the care of Rugaz Rescue, she had a very bad yeast infection in her ears. The canals were so swollen that we couldn't see inside. Meds reduced the swelling but that only revealed a bigger problem—Jaydee had giant masses in her ears; she was miserable. But...surgery to remove the masses only revealed many smaller masses beneath the big ones. We chose to continue the expensive medications as opposed to a $10,000 surgery to remove the ear canals, and finally, after many months, the vet could see in her ears. He said, "It is like seeing a cobblestone road...down her ear canals." It's been a long road for all of us, and after a year of loving and caring for Jaydee as a foster, would I let her go? I wouldn't hear of it. -*Sarah Bittenbender*

A Foster's Duty

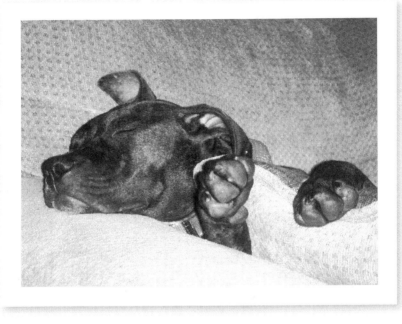

I took in my first foster dog from Rugaz Rescue and, thanks to my husband, became an instant foster failure (by keeping him). I was determined to not let that happen again and to be stronger with the next dog because if I failed twice, there would be no more "room at the inn" to help further dogs onto a better life.

Our second foster was Tazzy, who came barreling into our lives like the Tasmanian Devil. Little did I know what an effect this brindle girl would have on me. At first I wondered what I got myself into because she jumped on everything, chewed on everything, pooped on everything, and caused so much mayhem. However, as the weeks moved on I noticed she was eager to learn and do as I asked of her. Within weeks, every one of her bad behaviors was corrected, and she was acing basic obedience with little effort on my part. Tazzy now seemed determined to appreciate her new life, not taking anything for granted.

Brindles are not in high demand for adoption, and for four months *nobody* requested a meet-and-greet with her. I kept trying to tell people what an incredible girl she was and that whoever does finally come to meet her will fall instantly in love, but it wasn't until after forming a very deep, mutual bond that Tazzy got her big break at an adopt-a-thon.

Within one hour of arriving, Tazzy had three people interested in her, but I noticed myself giving negative information about her personality. I worried I was about to blow Tazzy's first chance to actually get adopted; that is, until the nicest looking family approached and made eye contact with her. I could tell right away that they were going to become her new forever home as they immediately fell for each other—which was exactly what I thought would happen when the right person came along.

Tazzy (now Roxy) lives with an incredible family who meets just about all my criteria: a dad, a stay-at-home mom, two kids, one dog, and lots of love. Yet here I am, still stalking her new mother's Facebook page in hopes that she will publish new photos of the dog I jokingly refer to as, "the one I let get away." Looking at Tazzy's pictures makes me smile with a tear in my eye because, though I am happy she found a forever family who absolutely adores her, her little paw prints will forever be engraved in my heart. Subsequent foster dogs simply haven't had the same impact.

I wrote the following poem to address a question often asked of foster families: "How can you spend so much time with a dog and then let her go?" My response is: "If those of us whose hearts break and tears fall for the dogs don't do it, who will?"

I've rescued some dogs, five with me right now; family and friends ask, "Why would she, and how?"

But each time I gaze deep into their eyes; their trust, love, forgiveness—I'm always surprised.

Their lives, love, allegiance, unconditional for me; I really don't mind if you don't get what I see.

Hearts of angels, so willing to please; abandoned, abused, infested with fleas.

One at a time, I'll let them into my heart; it's not a real lot, but I guess it's a start.

For those who will foster, be willing to cry; but for each who mans up, one less dog will die.

Tazzy's the first I have to let go; my commitment invested for another to know.

My original response, "I don't want the sorrow;" but had I stuck to my guns, she'd see no tomorrow.

I taught her some manners—to sit and obey; for the very first time she learned how to play.

She learned stay and down, to potty outside; to leave it and heel, I'm beaming with pride.

I've fed her and taught her to conquer her fears; all the joy she has brought us we'll cherish for years.

All this and more, she learned to please me; but for somebody else, a good girl she will be.

It's not easy to love her and then let her go; but if I stay strong, another dog saved I shall know.

My "Spazzy Razzama Tazzy" I'll never forget; tears of joy and sorrow, on your life you can bet.

God let them love her as much as I do; be kind and be patient, should she chew their shoe.

 *Angel Costanzo*

About Happy Tails Books™

Happy Tails Books™ was created to help support animal rescue efforts by showcasing the love, happiness, and joy adopted dogs have to offer. With the help of animal rescue groups, stories are submitted by people who have adopted dogs, and then Happy Tails Books™ compiles them into breed-specific books. These books serve not only to entertain, but also to educate readers about dog adoption and the characteristics of each specific type of dog. Happy Tails Books™ donates a significant portion of proceeds back to the rescue groups who help gather stories for the books.

 Happy Tails Books™

To submit a story or learn about other books Happy Tails Books™ publishes, please visit our website at http://happytailsbooks.com.

We're Writing Books about ALL of Your Favorite Dogs!

Schnauzer Chihuahua Golden Retriever PUG
DACHSHUND German Shepherd Collie Boxer
Labrador Retriever Husky Beagle ALL AMERICAN
Border Collie Pit Bull Terrier Shih Tzu Miniature Pinscher
Chow Chow Australian Shepherd Rottweiler Greyhound
Boston Terrier Jack Russell Poodle Cocker Spaniel
  Doberman Pinscher Yorkie SHEEPDOG
GREAT DANE ST. BERNARD Pointer Blue Heeler

Find Them at Happytailsbooks.com!

Make your dog famous!

Do you have a great story about your adopted dog? We are looking for stories, poems, and even your dog's favorite recipes to include on our website and in upcoming books! Please visit the website below for story guidelines and submission instructions. **http://happytailsbooks.com/ submit.htm**

Made in the USA
Lexington, KY
02 April 2013